SMART STRATEGIES FOR CHILD
RESILIENCE, COMMUNICATION,
AND PERSONAL GROWTH

THE PLAY THERAPY PLAYBOOK FOR PARENTS

100+ FUN-FILLED TECHNIQUES, TIPS, AND ACTIVITIES TO DEEPEN PARENT-CHILD CONNECTIONS

KRISSA LAINE

© **Copyright 2024 - All rights reserved.**

The content contained within this book may not be reproduced, duplicated, or transmitted without direct written permission from the author or the publisher.

Under no circumstances will any blame or legal responsibility be held against the publisher or author for any damages, reparation, or monetary loss due to the information contained within this book, either directly or indirectly.

Legal Notice:

This book is copyright-protected. It is only for personal use. You cannot amend, distribute, sell, use, quote, or paraphrase any part of this book's content without the author's or publisher's consent.

Disclaimer Notice:

Please note that the information contained within this document is for educational and entertainment purposes only. All effort has been executed to present accurate, up-to-date, reliable, and complete information. No warranties of any kind are declared or implied. Readers acknowledge that the author is not engaged in rendering legal, financial, medical, or professional advice. The content within this book has been derived from various sources. Please consult a licensed professional before attempting any techniques outlined in this book.

By reading this document, the reader agrees that under no circumstances is the author responsible for any direct or indirect losses incurred because of the use of the information contained within this document, including, but not limited to, errors, omissions, or inaccuracies.

Table of Contents

Introduction 5

Chapter 1: The Power of Play Therapy 7
    Play Therapy 7
    The Difference Between Traditional and Play Therapy 11
    Setting the Stage for Play Therapy 16

Chapter 2: Drawing and Painting Activities 21
    Benefits of Drawing and Painting 21
    Expressive Sketching 23
    Colorful Explorations 29
    Guided Art Narratives 35

Chapter 3: Constructing and Sculpting Activities 41
    Benefits of Constructing and Sculpting in Play Therapy 41
    Emotional Clay Modeling 44
    Building Emotional Structures 47
    Creative Recycling 52

Chapter 4: Crafts Activities 57
    Benefits of Crafting 57
    Emotion Crafting 58
    Vision Boards 62
    Memory and Experience Crafts 67

Chapter 5: Dancing and Music Activities 73
    Benefits of Dancing and Music 73
    Expressive Dance 74
    Rhythmic Emotions 79
    Explorative Singing 85

Chapter 6: Acting and Storytelling Activities 93
    Benefits of Acting and Storytelling... 93
    Emotion Role Play.. 95
    Therapeutic Puppetry.. 102
    Narrative Healing.. 107

Chapter 7: Digital Detox Activities................................... 113
    Identifying Screen Dependency.. 113
    Activities Away from Screens... 115

Chapter 8: Self-Control and Concentration Activities 129
    Benefits of Boosting Self-Control... 129
    Mindfulness Activities 130
    Focus-Based Games.. 137
    Emotional Regulation Strategies... 142

Conclusion 149

Techniques, Tips, & Activities Recap 151

References... 167

Exclusive Bonuses 169

Introduction

Parenting is like assembling a puzzle without the cover image to guide you. Each child, each emotion, and each challenge is a unique piece, and finding where each fits can often leave you feeling overwhelmed and lost.

When I first held my twins, tiny fingers clutching onto mine, I was flooded with emotions—love, wonder, and the overwhelming weight of responsibility. In connecting to my children's world, playing became the bridge. Through drawing, dancing, storytelling, and even crafting, I discovered a language rich in emotion and insight. All these experiences, learnings, and heartfelt moments are poured into these pages to share with you.

Every chapter of this book and every activity suggested stems from an academic understanding as a psychology major and real-world experience as a mom. As you delve deeper, you will find 100+ techniques, strategies, and activities that uncover the magic play therapy brings to your child's life and your relationship. The bond you forge, the moments you share, and the emotions you explore together will be your reward.

Chapter 1
The Power of Play Therapy

Play is the language of childhood. For young minds, it is much more than fun and games. Playing allows children to explore their innermost feelings, make sense of complex situations, and find solutions to problems through imagination. This innate power of play to heal, teach, and transform is what play therapy taps into. In this profoundly effective therapeutic approach, toys become the words, blocks turn into bridges between the internal and external, and games morph into gateways to gain mastery over emotions.

This chapter will explore how play therapy provides the perfect backdrop for children to freely express their inner struggles, safely work through trauma, boost self-esteem, and build coping mechanisms. Comprehend the immense benefits and the difference between play therapy and traditional counseling.

Play Therapy

From building sandcastles to role-playing with dolls, children use play as a natural method to explore, communicate, and understand the world around them. Play therapy uses play as a means for children to express themselves, confront their fears, and address traumatic events. It provides a safe and familiar environment for children to *"speak"* in a language they know best: the language of play.

Every parent has witnessed the spontaneous imagination of a child during play. A child may pretend a cardboard box is a spaceship or that the teddy bear is sick and needs to see a doctor. These plays are a window into children's minds, emotions, and overall well-being.

Imagine a young girl who has recently moved to a new city. She might role-play situations where her toys are feeling lost or trying to make new friends. Through these scenarios, she explores her feelings about the move and tries to make sense of them.

Children may not have the vocabulary or emotional maturity to express their feelings, but play offers an alternative. It acts as a bridge between their inner emotions and the external world, allowing them to process events or feelings they might not otherwise be able to express.

The Therapeutic Power of Play

Play therapy, a therapeutic approach designed especially for children recognizes the influence play has on a child's development. It takes the innate power of play as a medium for healing, understanding, and growth. Look into the multifaceted benefits of this therapeutic approach below.

Safe Expression and Emotion Regulation

Many children struggle to articulate complex emotions. Some may lack the vocabulary, feel overwhelmed, or unsure how their feelings will be received. Play therapy provides these children with a nurturing environment where they can express themselves without pressure to get it right.

Toys, drawings, and ***games*** in play therapy become vehicles for emotion. Children communicate their innermost feelings, fears, and thoughts by selecting toys or drawing particular images. Once you have understood the nuances of children's play, you can interpret these actions, helping to unravel the child's emotional world.

Emotional regulation is an essential life skill too. Play therapy provides children with a platform to identify various emotions and practice managing them. Experimenting with reactions to different scenarios became possible, helping them better understand and control their feelings.

Introduce coping strategies during the activity if a child gets frustrated easily. Over time, the child learns to apply these strategies in real-life situations.

Building Coping Mechanisms

Children, much like adults, face a multitude of challenges. What play therapy offers is a controlled environment where they can confront these challenges, experiment with solutions, and develop coping mechanisms.

When children simulate scenarios, confront imaginary monsters, or navigate the playground's social dynamics, they are essentially practicing. Each repetition, with gentle guidance, allows them to build resilience and problem-solving skills.

A child anxious about starting a new school might create a play scenario with dolls going to school for the first time. Through this enactment, they can explore various outcomes, preparing them emotionally for the upcoming change.

Strengthening Relationships

By involving parents, caregivers, or even siblings in some sessions, play therapy can bridge communication gaps and enhance familial bonds. Children often play out real-life scenarios, mirroring their experiences. Doing so offers a unique insight for parents to see the world through their child's eyes. It can also pave the way for addressing misunderstandings or conflicts in a supportive setting.

Enhancing Self-Esteem

A child who feels overshadowed by a sibling might take the lead in a play scenario, demonstrating leadership and decision-making. Such experiences can instill a sense of accomplishment and boost their self-esteem. This is an example of how children often face challenges that might diminish their sense of self-worth. Through play therapy, they can explore achievements, overcome obstacles, and manifest success stories, all of which contribute to a positive self-image.

Improving Communication Skills

Through play, children can hone their verbal and non-verbal communication skills. As they interact with toys or other participants, they learn to convey their ideas, listen to others, and build a vocabulary for their emotions. Take role-playing games, for instance. Here, a child has to express the feelings of a character, which can encourage them to articulate emotions they had not previously been able to express.

Enhancing Problem-Solving Abilities

Play therapy often involves scenarios where a child faces a challenge or conflict. They can explore different solutions, weigh outcomes, and decide on the best course of action, refining their problem-solving skills.

Providing a Sense of Mastery and Control

Children, especially those who have experienced trauma or upheaval, can often feel that they have little control over their lives. Play therapy allows them to be in charge, make decisions, and effect outcomes, restoring a sense of control and agency.

The Difference Between Traditional and Play Therapy

Play therapy and traditional counseling are two common approaches used to help children cope with emotional issues. While both can be effective, there are important differences between these therapeutic techniques. Understanding the key distinctions between traditional and play therapy helps determine the type most beneficial for your child.

Traditional Therapy

Traditional therapy, often referred to as talk therapy or counseling, is a form of psychotherapy that hinges on verbal communication. During this structured process, therapists and clients engage in conversations to explore and address emotional, psychological, and behavioral challenges.

In a typical traditional therapy session, the therapist creates a safe, confidential space, encouraging the individual to speak about their feelings, thoughts, and experiences. Then, they listen actively, offering feedback, insights, and coping strategies. Various therapeutic techniques may be utilized, such as Cognitive Behavioral Therapy (CBT), which focuses on identifying and challenging negative thought patterns, or Psychoanalysis, which delves deeper into past experiences and subconscious thoughts.

For children, traditional therapy helps articulate feelings, process events, and develop coping mechanisms. Usually, this therapy is chosen for older children or adolescents who can express themselves verbally and comprehend abstract concepts. However, other therapeutic methods, like play therapy, are more effective for younger children who find continuous conversation challenging or intimidating.

Differences and Similarities

The most obvious difference between play therapy and traditional counseling is the use of play and toys during the sessions. Play therapy utilizes a child's natural inclination for play to help them express feelings and process experiences. Rather than sitting face-to-face and talking with a therapist, children are encouraged to use toys, art supplies, sand trays, and other items to work through issues creatively. Doing so provides a way for kids to communicate that feels natural and comfortable. Here, play is the primary way of communicating. Instead of a direct conversation, a child in play therapy uses toys and other *"play"* activities, indirectly shedding light on their emotions.

In contrast, traditional counseling typically involves mostly talking and verbal processing. While counselors may incorporate some playful elements, the primary mode of therapy is through conversation. Children are encouraged to openly discuss their thoughts, feelings, and experiences with the counselor. Therapists converse with the child, gently probing and exploring their world of thoughts, emotions, and behaviors. For instance, a child grappling with a recent family move might be prompted to directly discuss their feelings and reactions.

Despite the different approaches, play therapy and counseling aim to achieve similar goals. These include helping children cope with difficult emotions, process trauma, improve social skills, build self-esteem, and strengthen the parent-child relationship. The main priority for any therapy is creating an environment where the child feels safe and supported.

While traditional counseling might resonate more with older children capable of articulating their feelings, play therapy often finds its audience in younger children, usually between the ages of 3 and 12.

Keep in mind that both play therapy and traditional counseling provide meaningful ways to help children manage emotional struggles. While their approaches differ, the goal remains to build coping skills, resilience, and a positive outlook. By understanding the key differences and benefits of each type of therapy, you can make the optimal choice to help your child heal and thrive. Most of all, the supportive presence of a caring therapist gives children the space to explore their inner world, setting them on the path to leading happier, healthier lives.

Picking Which Approach

In the complex tapestry of therapeutic approaches for children, two distinct threads weave into the fabric of healing and growth: play therapy and traditional counseling. Each approach possesses unique qualities, offering its own set of pros and cons. Choosing these two paths can be empowering and perplexing as a parent, caregiver, or therapist.

Pros and Cons of Traditional Counseling

Traditional counseling offers its own set of pros and cons that you should take note of:

Pros:
- Talking directly allows children to process thoughts and emotions through language.

- The therapist can provide guidance, insight, and coping strategies through discussion.
- Children learn to confidently express themselves verbally.
- Counseling may help resolve some concrete issues more directly.

Cons:
- Younger children may lack the verbal skills and maturity for talk therapy.
- The office setting feels formal and intimidating to some kids.
- Children may have trouble opening up about sensitive topics through talking alone.
- Counseling depends heavily on the child's willingness and ability to discuss their inner world.

Pros and Cons of Play Therapy

Play therapy offers several advantages that make it well-suited for working with children:

- It aligns with a child's natural mode of expression through play. Therapy feels less intimidating and more engaging for kids.
- Physical toys and activities help children tap into emotions and experiences that may be difficult to express verbally.
- Play therapy encourages creativity and imagination as outlets for processing inner struggles.
- Children tend to be more open and comfortable expressing themselves through play.
- It allows the therapist or parents to understand a child's inner world.
- Parents can also participate in sessions to strengthen their bond with their children.

However, there are some potential downsides to play therapy:

- Some children may have trouble accessing emotions through play alone.
- Parents may need extra guidance to understand the symbolic meaning behind their children's play themes.
- Results may take longer to achieve than counseling.

When to Choose Play Therapy

Play therapy tends to be the preferred approach if your child:

- **Is young or has limited verbal skills.** Play provides a developmentally appropriate outlet for expression.
- **Has experienced trauma.** Play helps kids process traumatic memories and feelings in a safe, indirect way.
- **Struggles with social skills.** Play sessions teach essential skills like cooperation, communication, and self-regulation.
- **Is extremely shy, anxious, or reluctant to talk openly.** Play helps build trust at the child's own pace.
- **Needs help managing big emotions like anger, fear, or sadness.** Play provides a constructive outlet for releasing and coping with these feelings.
- **Is coping with life changes like divorce or a move.** Play allows kids to work through confusion, worry, grief, and other challenging transitions.

While every child is unique, play therapy is often a good fit when addressing social-emotional struggles, trauma, family changes, and other common issues impacting younger kids. However, traditional talk therapy may be optimal for teens who need help developing insight through in-depth discussions. Most importantly, seek input from experienced child therapists when determining the best approach for your child's needs.

Setting the Stage for Play Therapy

The transformative power of play therapy is undeniable. *But how does one set the stage to unlock its potential?* Like planting a seed requires the right soil, nurturing conditions, and a gentle introduction to its new environment, play therapy also requires a carefully crafted setting. Explore how to create that perfect atmosphere, ensuring children benefit the most from this therapeutic approach.

Creating a Safe Environment

One of the primary pillars of play therapy's success is the environment in which it is conducted. Create a sanctuary where children can freely explore their emotions.

Physical Safety

Every child, when entering a new space, first gauges its safety. Some things to take note of include the following:

- **Cleanliness:** A clean room minimizes health risks and conveys care and professionalism. Regularly sanitize toys and play materials and maintain an organized space.
- **Child-Friendly Infrastructure:** Furniture should be appropriate in size, devoid of sharp edges, and stable, preventing tipping over. Ensure that shelves or wall hangings are securely fixed and cannot be easily pulled down.
- **Safety Checks:** Regularly inspect toys for breakages. A broken toy can have sharp edges, posing a risk. Ensure that small toy parts, which can be a choking hazard, are promptly addressed.

Emotional Safety

Beyond the physical realm, the emotional ambiance of the therapy room plays a role in a child's comfort and openness. Follow these tips to ensure emotional safety:

- **Warmth and Welcome:** The room decor should resonate with warmth. Soft lighting, from floor lamps or string lights, creates a serene ambiance. Calming colors like blues, greens, or pastels can evoke a sense of tranquility.
- **Minimize Distractions:** The therapy room should be a cocoon, shielding the child from external disturbances. This means no sudden noises or visual stimuli that might jolt them out of their exploratory zone. A simple curtain or blind can dim bright sunlight, and soft background music or white noise machines can muffle external sounds.
- **Personal Touch:** Have a space where children can store their creations or favorite toys. This personalized touch can make them feel valued and establish continuity between sessions.

Privacy and Boundaries

For a child to truly open up, they need to trust you and the environment. To foster trust, do the following:

- **Confidential Space:** Ensure the therapy room is well insulated from external noise, assuring the child that their conversations will not be overheard. A simple sign outside the door indicating a session is in progress can prevent accidental interruptions.
- **Setting Expectations:** At the outset, explain the concept of confidentiality to the child. Let them know that what they say or do in this room is a shared secret, only to be divulged to others if there is a concern for their well-being.

- **Respecting Personal Space:** Every child has a different comfort level regarding personal space. Some might be okay with a reassuring pat, while others might not want to be touched. Respect these boundaries, always seeking consent before initiating any physical contact.

Introducing Children to the Concept

Play therapy can be an unfamiliar territory for children. When guiding them towards it, make their first steps into this new realm gentle, comforting, and transparent, setting the tone for a positive and therapeutic experience.

Use Simple Language

Children tend to feel apprehensive about what they do not understand. Using language that resonates with their world can dispel many of these uncertainties. Instead of inundating them with therapeutic jargon, liken play therapy to elements they are already familiar with. For instance, describe it as a special playdate or a unique show-and-tell session where toys and drawings help share their stories. Emphasizing that this is their time and there is no right or wrong way to express themselves can offer them reassurance and a sense of ownership.

Address Their Concerns

Children may come into play therapy with preconceived notions, perhaps influenced by peers or snippets of information they have picked up. Addressing their concerns head-on fosters an atmosphere of trust. Initiate an open dialogue where they can voice any questions or misgivings. Providing clear, age-appropriate answers also ensures they feel heard and validated. Sometimes, using relatable stories or characters can be an effective way to explain play therapy. Narrating how a beloved character from a storybook or TV show also talked to someone when they felt upset or confused can make the concept more tangible and relatable for the child.

Engage in Parallel Play

For some children, especially those who are more reserved or anxious, diving straight into therapeutic play may be overwhelming. Parallel play offers a softer introduction. Engage in independent play to demonstrate how to use the available materials, which often piques the child's interest and encourages them to join. Following your lead ensures they remain comfortable and in control. For instance, if a child shows interest in a specific toy, such as a dollhouse, start by setting up a scene, inviting your kid to add characters, or narrating a story. Therapeutic elements can be subtly woven as their comfort grows, guiding their play toward more expressive and healing avenues.

Chapter 2
Drawing and Painting Activities

From the scribbled masterpieces of toddlers to the refined techniques of older children, the simple acts of drawing and painting hold an unparalleled power to enrich young lives. These creative endeavors offer children an infinite portal to self-expression, emotional regulation, enhanced cognitive skills, and much more.

Equipped with a basic understanding of drawing and painting multifaceted benefits, incorporate such activities in this chapter into your children's routines in ways that empower, soothe, and inspire.

Benefits of Drawing and Painting

Drawing and painting are two of the most effective and versatile tools in play therapy activities. These two have various, such as:

Enhancing Motor Skills

Motor skills are the abilities that support movement and coordination. As children grow, they undergo a phase where these abilities undergo rapid advancement. Drawing and painting activities are the most organic ways to nurture and refine these skills.

Take a moment to observe a young child with a crayon in their hand. Maintaining a grip or a preschooler's earnest effort to draw a straight line speaks volumes about their developmental journey. Though such activities might be rudimentary to adults, they hold significant value for children. These seemingly basic tasks lay the groundwork for fine motor development. Children unknowingly work on finger agility and hone hand-eye coordination with each brush stroke, doodle, or intricate drawing.

Promoting Emotional Catharsis

Art, particularly drawing and painting, opens avenues for profound emotional expression. These activities are particularly potent in providing emotional relief, especially within therapeutic contexts.

Children face challenges like adults, from past traumas to overwhelming feelings. For many, articulating these intense emotions verbally can be daunting. However, drawing grants children a voice without the need for words. For instance, a canvas covered in shades of dark blue and gray depicting a tumultuous sky might be a child's way of conveying anger or sadness. On the other hand, a scene filled with soft pastels could symbolize moments of joy or contentment. Essentially, the artwork becomes a silent testament, a diary capturing the ebbs and flows of their emotional state.

Boosting Creativity and Imagination

Drawing and painting are gateways to the boundless realms of creativity and imagination. These mediums offer children a unique platform to dive deep into their imaginative worlds, uninhibited and free.

In today's age, where screens and digital distractions are ever-present, the simplicity and allure of drawing and painting come forth as a rejuvenating alternative. These activities propel children to break the mold, to conceptualize and birth ideas entirely on their own. For example, the idea of an underwater-residing cat or a tree sprouting delightful cupcakes might seem unbelievable, but for a child, it is a testament to their uninhibited creativity. In the universe of art, boundaries blur, and the only constant is the infinity of possibilities.

Expressive Sketching

A child's mind is a vibrant mix of dreams, emotions, and sanctuaries. Through expressive sketching, you journey into these intricate patterns, unveiling the silent stories that your little ones harbor. With the tender strokes that capture their safest hideaways, the vivid colors that mirror their swirling emotions, or the imaginative lines that trace their nocturnal journeys, sketching becomes more than art. It transforms into a voice, a dialogue, a bridge connecting their internal world to the canvas of reality.

My Safe Space

Picture a moment when your child seems overwhelmed, where the weight of the world appears too heavy on their tiny shoulders. In such moments, they often retreat into their world, seeking solace in their thoughts. Expressive sketching will help children identify, articulate, and visually capture their safe havens. Whether a snug corner of their room, a grandparent's lap, or even an enchanting castle floating amidst clouds, every child has a place where worries melt away.

Objective:
- To identify surroundings and items that bring comfort and security.
- To express emotions through creative means.
- To cultivate calming techniques for anxiety or emotional turmoil.

Best Suited For:
Such activity works well when a child is dealing with stressful events or changes causing worry, sadness, or frustration. It can be used proactively to build coping skills or, at the moment, to soothe big emotions. Best for ages 4 to 9.

Materials Needed:
- Paper
- Crayons, colored pencils, or markers
- Optional: magazines, glue, safety scissors for collage elements

Instructions:
1. **Explain to your child that everyone needs a safe and cozy place when worried, angry, or sad.** This special place makes us feel better and helps big feelings go away.
2. **Ask your child to close their eyes and think of their favorite place to be when they need comfort or quiet time.** *Where is it? What does it look like? What special things are there?*
3. **After thinking for a minute or two, have them draw a picture of their safe place, including as much detail as possible.** Encourage them to use their imagination to add anything that makes them feel warm, cozy, and cared for.
4. **Once finished, invite your child to walk you through their drawing and describe their safe place.** Use open-ended questions to understand what specific elements bring them comfort or joy.

    Sample questions:
    - *What did you draw in your special safe place?*
    - *Why did you choose this place?*
    - *How does this place make you feel when you go here?*

- ○ *If you could bring anything with you here, what would you bring?*
- ○ *Is there anyone you want to be in your safe place?*

5. **Consider cutting out magazine pictures of items representing their safe place for an added sensory element.** Have your child create a collage by gluing these pictures onto their original drawing.

Processing the Activity
- Discuss how everyone needs a safe place to go that is filled with things that make them feel cared for.
- When they feel worried or upset, prompt them to think of their safe place drawing. Taking deep breaths while picturing it can be calming.
- Designate a physical *"safe spot"* related to their drawing in your home, like a comfy bean bag chair with favorite stuffed animals.
- Turn their drawing into a visualization exercise. Have your child close their eyes while you verbally guide them through imagining each detail of their safe place for relaxation.
- Let your child decorate the picture and place it somewhere visible to remind them of their coping strategy when big emotions come up.
- Share that you have a safe place, too. Describe yours and talk about how you use this coping strategy when needed.

Emotion Faces

Remember when your little one could not quite put their feelings into words? Or those days when new, overwhelming emotions took over? Maybe it was just a regular school day, learning about emotions with peers. During these pivotal moments, this kind of activity shines bright, bridging their heartbeats and art pieces, making emotions a touchable, seeable, and understandable part of their world.

Objective:
- To expand emotional vocabulary and recognition skills.
- To increase understanding of how feelings manifest physically through facial expressions.
- To use creativity as an outlet for articulating internal emotional states.

Best Suited For:
Works well for children who have difficulty identifying and expressing emotions verbally. It also helps build empathy for how others feel. Best for ages 4 to 8.

Materials:
- Blank sheets of paper *(preferably larger size for more space)*.
- Pencils, crayons, colored pencils, or markers.
- Printed reference sheets or cards depicting various emotions *(optional)*.
- A quiet, comfortable space to sit and draw.

Instructions:
1. **Ensure the environment is calm and free from distractions.** Doing so will help the child focus and engage fully in the activity.
2. **Start a conversation about feelings.** Say, *"Everyone feels different things at different times. Sometimes, you feel happy, sad, and even angry or surprised. Today, we are going to draw some of those feelings."*
3. **Hand the child a blank sheet of paper and drawing materials.** Ask them to think about a time they felt really happy. *What did that happiness look like on their face?* Prompt them to draw that happy face.

4. **Repeat the process for other emotions like sadness, anger, surprise, etc.** Between each emotion, discuss scenarios when they might have felt this way. For example, *"Remember when we couldn't go to the park because it was raining? How did that make you feel?"*
5. **If the child struggles to depict a certain emotion, show them the reference cards.** Discuss the features of each face—for instance, *"See how the eyebrows are drawn downward and the mouth turns up? That is how some people look when angry."*

Processing the Activity:
- Once all the drawings are complete, lay them out and review them together. Ask open-ended questions such as, *"Which of these faces was the easiest for you to draw? Which was the hardest? Why?"*
- Encourage the child to label each face with the emotion it represents, enhancing their emotional lexicon.
- Discuss how other people might feel in various situations, using the drawings as a reference. For instance, *"How do you think your friend felt when she lost her toy? Can you point to one of your emotional faces that might show how she felt?"*
- Conclude the activity by discussing positive emotions and actions that can be taken when feeling negative.

Illustrating Dreamscapes

Likely, you witnessed your child waking up from a nap with eyes shimmering with remnants of a dream, trying to piece together the fragments of their nighttime adventure. Sometimes, these dreams are painted with hues of joy, while other times, they might carry tints of confusion or even fear. *"Illustrating Dreamscapes"* is a crafted expedition into the subconscious. By encouraging children to bring these dreams to life on paper, fortify their imaginative prowess, and provide a platform to discuss and even unravel the cryptic messages of their dreams.

Objective:
- To guide children in visually capturing their dream experiences.
- To nurture their creativity.
- To allow dream sequences to bolster the child's creative spirit when brought to life on paper.

When is this activity best suited to do?
Consider doing this activity when your child appears eager to share or puzzled by a recent dream. Being distressed upon waking could indicate they experienced a nightmare. Utilize it too when your child is simply in a creative mood, eager to plunge into the depths of their imagination.

Materials:
- Large blank sheets of paper or sketchbooks.
- Drawing tools: *Pencils, crayons, colored pencils, markers,* or even *watercolors for a more fluid representation.*
- A quiet, serene workspace imbued with a sense of comfort.

Instructions:
1. Ensure the environment is calm and free from disruptions. A peaceful setting aids in recollection and creativity.
2. Start by asking gently, *"Did you have a dream last night? Or is there a dream you remember and would like to share?"*
3. Hand over the drawing materials, allowing them to depict their dream without inhibitions. Your role is to be an observer and supporter, resisting the urge to guide or interrupt their process.
4. Encourage imaginative storytelling when they cannot recall a recent dream or prefer to craft one. *"What would it be if you could dream about anything tonight?"*

Processing the Activity:
- Once their masterpiece is complete, delve into a discussion. *"Can you tell me the story behind this drawing? What happened in this dream?"*
- Navigate the emotional terrain of their dream. *"How did you feel during this dream? Were there parts that made you happy or scared?"*
- Gently probe if elements of the dream resonate with real-life events. *"Does this dream remind you of something that happened recently?"*
- If the dream was distressing, offer comfort. *"Remember, dreams cannot hurt you. I am here with you."*
- Consider creating a *'Dream Journal'* where they can store these drawings. Over time, revisiting these can be both fun and insightful.

Colorful Explorations

In the vast canvas of life, colors dance with emotion, rhythm, and identity. Much like the splendor of a rainbow following a rainstorm, children embody a radiant spectrum of emotions, experiences, and unique characteristics that shape their essence. Within play therapy, colorful explorations dive deep into this vibrant world, unraveling the layers of a child's day, their sense of self, and their perspective on the world around them. As they dabble in hues, blend shades, and paint their stories, each child embarks on self-discovery, learns the magic of unity in diversity, and appreciates the harmonious symphony of their daily life.

Rainbow of Me

Step outside on a rainy day, and you might be lucky to witness a rainbow. With its array of colors, each arc of a rainbow tells a unique story of the sun and rain in harmonious interplay. Much like a rainbow, every child is a mixture of various hues—each shade representing their emotions, experiences, and traits. This therapeutic and interactive activity is designed to enable children to reflect, recognize, and cherish their multifaceted personalities.

Objective:
- To enhance self-awareness and bolster self-esteem by helping children visually capture the myriad aspects of their identity.
- To celebrate the distinctive traits, memories, and roles that sculpt each child's persona.

Best Suited For:
When you notice your child grappling with self-doubt or find it challenging to voice their strengths, do this activity. Crafted for youngsters aged 5 to 9.

Materials Needed:
1. Horizontal white paper sheets.
2. Vivid markers, crayons, or colored pencils represent the rainbow spectrum.
3. Optional enhancements: collage essentials like magazines, scissors, and adhesive.

The Rainbow of Me Activity:
1. Hand over the white sheet to your child. Direct them to draw a black arch, signifying the crest of a rainbow originating from soft clouds.
2. Dive deep into the analogy: as every rainbow is unique, so are they. Craft a rainbow reflecting their persona's varied hues. Assure them of the absence of any *'right'* or *'wrong'* method.
3. Offer them a moment of introspection. If they seem hesitant, sprinkle in queries:
   - *"Which hue resonates with your personality today?"*
   - *"What shade screams 'YOU'?"*

- *"Which color mirrors your joy?"*
4. As they breathe life into the rainbow with their selected colors, they engage in conversations about the symbolism of each band.
5. For a touch of creativity, incorporate magazine cut-outs that resonate with your child's chosen colors, representing their passions, memories, or strengths.
6. Progress layer by layer until the rainbow authentically showcases their diverse identity.

Processing the Activity:
- Initiate a walkthrough of their masterpiece, nudging them to detail the essence of every hue.
- Dwell on the thought that our individualities are as unique and precious as rainbows. Every color adds depth to who we are.
- For mature kids, correlate the colors to the virtues and qualities they outlined.
- Muse on the concept of evolving life experiences, adding richness to their identities, akin to a rainbow's ever-changing hues.
- Showcase their artistic endeavor and revisit it when the world gets too loud, reminding them of their inner radiance.

My Day in Colors

Children thrive on routines and rhythms throughout their day. Use color as a creative medium to help your kid reflect on their daily schedules from start to finish. Illustrating different times of their day in color builds time awareness while enabling self-expression.

Objective:
- To cultivate a structured sense of daily rhythms and routines.

- To boost comprehension of time sequencing and transitions.
- To encourage reflection on activities or emotions associated with different times of day.

Best Suited For:
Works well for children who struggle with transitions, following schedules, or general time awareness. It also helps identify times of day that may be stressful or comforting. Best for ages 4 to 8.

Materials Needed:
- White paper or cardstock cut to represent a sunrise and sunset
- Crayons, colored pencils, or markers
- Clock with movable hands *(optional)*

Instructions:
1. Cut paper to resemble a sunrise on one side, fading to a sunset on the opposite side. Explain this represents the full day from morning to bedtime.
2. Ask your child to think through a typical day from when they wake up to bedtime. Use a clock face to demonstrate the continuous progression of time if needed.
3. Have them divide the sunrise-sunset paper into sections representing different times or activities in their daily schedule. Label each section, covering morning, afternoon, evening, and bedtime routines.
4. Instruct your child to use colors to illustrate each segmented time of day. Ask:
    - *What color matches the feeling of waking up in the morning? And eating breakfast?*
    - *What color fits your mood when playing outside vs. doing homework?*
    - *What color represents the end of school and transition to family time in the evenings?*

- *What color helps you feel calm and sleepy at bedtime?*
5. Encourage them to cover each section using crayons or colored pencils in the colors they associate with that time of day. The colors should reflect their typical mood and activities during each routine.
6. When finished, have them walk you through their daily color chart from start to finish, explaining why they chose those hues.

Processing the Activity:
- **Discuss how routines create a sense of safety and predictability.** The colors represent visual cues about what happens when.
- **Note the use of soothing colors during challenging times like school or bedtime.** Talk about how we can purposefully surround ourselves with calming colors.
- **Identify any lengthy white spaces lacking color.** These may represent unstructured times needing more routine. Work together to add color or activities.
- **Ask how they feel during stressful color segments.** Provide emotional labels if needed. Discuss preferred coping colors.
- **Post their daily color chart on the fridge to reinforce sequencing.** Refer to it when prepping for transitions.

Color Mixing Magic

Blending primary colors to make new hues inspires creativity while teaching the science of color theory. This activity uses hands-on color mixing to showcase how combining different elements can create beauty. It provides a valuable lesson about embracing diversity, as the colors are created to remind everyone to celebrate their unique spirit. This ignites creativity while teaching that wonderful things can happen when we combine ingredients in new ways.

Objective:
- To teach color theory by actively mixing primary colors.
- To demonstrate how combining unique ingredients makes something new.
- To use color as a metaphor for embracing human diversity and inclusion.

Best Suited For:
Works well alongside lessons about family diversity, culture, or race. It also benefits anxious children who worry about differences. Best for ages 5 to 8.

Materials Needed:
- Red, blue, and yellow paint, food coloring, or dye
- Paintbrushes, droppers, or spoons for mixing
- Containers for blended colors
- White paper for color testing

The Color Mixing Activity:
1. Explain primary colors are like the main ingredients that all other colors come from. Have your child identify the primary colors red, blue, and yellow.
2. Have them use droppers or paintbrushes on a white palette or plate to add drops of the primary colors without mixing. Talk about how each remains vivid on its own.
3. Demonstrate mixing two colors at a time. Add some yellow to red, and green appears. Mix blue into yellow and see green again. Combine red and blue to make purple.
4. With each new blend, prompt your child to identify the resulting secondary color and describe how the blend looks brighter, darker, or more muted.
5. Take turns experimenting with blending primary colors freely using the paint palette. There are no rules; mix and observe the results!

6. As they create new hues, ask open questions to build color recognition. *What two colors made orange? Does adding more red or yellow change it?*
7. Allow your child to test their custom mixed colors by painting sample swatches on white paper. Add labels if desired.

Processing the Activity:
- Discuss how every unique color came from the three main primaries. Relate this to how combining different people creates diverse families, schools, and communities.
- Note how blending lightens or darkens shades. Draw parallels to how our experiences shape us while our core selves remain.
- Talk about appreciating all colors, light and dark. Similarly, fair and just communities value all people and perspectives.
- When conflicts about diversity arise, gently recall how colors combine beautifully into new expressions.

Guided Art Narratives

Art narratives in play therapy invite your little dreamers to embark on a heartfelt journey, retracing the footprints of cherished memories, envisioning their brightest aspirations, and weaving tales of fantastical beings. As each brushstroke unfolds a chapter, children hone their listening and creative visualization skills and unravel the intricate tapestries of their emotions, aspirations, and identities.

My Future Vision

Hopes and dreams about the future spark children's imagination and optimism. This activity encourages kids to depict their ideal future selves through art, building self-esteem and goal-setting skills.

Objective:
- To foster a positive outlook by envisioning desired future goals or achievements.
- To practice creative visualization as a motivational tool.
- To identify personal hopes and dreams as inspiration for purposeful goal-setting.

Best Suited For:
Benefits children who feel aimless, discouraged, or pessimistic about their potential. Ideal for ages 6 to 9 when goal-planning skills develop.

Materials Needed:
- Paper, canvas, or cardboard for painting
- Variety of art supplies like paint, crayons, magazines, glue
- Timer or calm music *(optional)*

Instructions:
1. Explain that picturing goals makes us feel hopeful and gives us purpose. Dreams about our future selves can inspire us.
2. Ask your child to close their eyes and imagine where they want to be someday. *Do they dream of a certain career or accomplishment? Where do they live? What are they proudest of?*
3. After a minute of guided visualization, have them open their eyes and describe their future vision in detail. *What did they see, hear, feel?*
4. Provide art supplies so they can illustrate this imagined future self-portrait and bring their dreams to life visually.
5. Encourage them to include symbols or words representing their hopes, talents, and values they want their future self to embody.
6. Play calm music or set a timer for 10 to 15 minutes so they can focus fully on visually depicting their most inspiring future.

7. When finished, have them walk you through their dream vision artwork and explain the goals and wishes it represents.

Processing the Activity:
- Identify short-term goals that can launch them toward their depicted vision. Make an achievable plan.
- When they feel discouraged, revisit their future vision as motivation to keep progressing.
- Schedule time to re-imagine and update their portrait as goals evolve with age.
- Display their artwork prominently as a reminder to remember their long-term aspirations daily.

Memory Recall

Reliving cherished memories together through art strengthens family bonds and fosters positive reminiscence. This activity invites children to illustrate special shared experiences after hearing the story told, enriching the memory's meaning. Recreating special memories through art allows children to immerse themselves in meaningful shared experiences. Deepening family bonds through positive reminiscing provides continuity and comfort during difficult transitions in life.

Objective:
- To deepen connections and family identity by recreating meaningful shared memories.
- To practice attentive listening skills.
- To build personal reflection through artistic expression.

Best Suited For:
Ideal for grieving or changing families wanting to honor past joyful times together before a loss or transition occurs. Great for ages 4 to 8.

Materials Needed:
- Drawing paper or canvas
- Markers, crayons, paints
- Photos or mementos to spark memories *(optional)*

Instructions:
1. Select a meaningful or humorous family memory to narrate to your child. For example, tell the story of a special beach vacation, holiday, or sibling's birth.
2. As you narrate the memory slowly, invite your child to close their eyes and vividly imagine the people, places, sights, smells, and feelings you describe.
3. After completely retelling the memory, ask your child to open their eyes and recount everything they pictured. Clarify details as needed.
4. Provide drawing materials and invite them to illustrate the special shared memory based on your narration and their mental envisioning. Remind them to include every element they can recall.
5. Offer prompts if they get stuck:
   - *What color was the sky? What shapes did you see?*
   - *What clothes were people wearing? What food did you eat?*
   - *What landmark or location stood out most?*
6. When finished, have them walk you through their memory drawing, prompting more sensory descriptions about the imagery and emotion captured.

Processing the Activity:
- Over time, repeat this activity, recalling other meaningful shared experiences to recreate.
- Compile the memory drawings into a cherished scrapbook or album to revisit.
- When facing present-day challenges, gently look back on joyful times together depicted in the drawings as comfort.

Character Creations

Inventing and portraying fictional personalities stimulates children's imagination and storytelling abilities. This activity invites them to visualize and draw whimsical characters based on verbal descriptions. Giving children creative license to create new identities stretches their imagination and builds empathy. Whimsical character invention also provides a safe outlet for expressing emotions and exploring new ways of being.

Objective:
- To practice attentive listening and translation of words into visuals.
- To build imagination and creativity through character invention.
- To gain emotional insight through the personalities invented.

Best Suited For:
Beneficial for shy or anxious children who want to explore bolder, more confident personas. It also helps kids cope with changes and express feelings through invented identities. Great for ages 5 to 8.

Materials Needed:
- Drawing paper, canvas, or cardboard
- Variety of art media like markers, paint, fabric, pipe cleaners
- Optional props like hats, glasses, or gloves for character inspiration

Instructions:
1. Provide a variety of art supplies and invite your child to invent a new character. Explain they can make the character look any way they want.

2. If they need inspiration, verbally describe potential personalities, hobbies, or quirks and have your child visualize the character as you speak.
    - For example: *"Catrina is a space explorer who wears a purple striped spacesuit and helmet with star stickers. She finds rare space gems on faraway planets."*
3. Allow plenty of time for your child to draw and decorate the character in detail based on the verbal description or their invention. Remind them to include distinct props and personality clues.
4. Introduce *"plot twists"* that prompt them to evolve the character. For Catrina, say she adopts a space puppy or gets a new space jetpack from alien friends.
5. Have your child introduce the invented character by sharing their name, backstory, personality, and other narrative details.

Processing the Activity:
- Continue inventing new *"friends"* with diverse appearances, cultures, abilities, and backgrounds.
- If any negative play arises related to differences, gently redirect the focus to cooperation and celebrating uniqueness.
- Note any feelings or struggles expressed subtly through the characters. Use pretend play to resolve imaginary conflicts.

Chapter 3
Constructing and Sculpting Activities

Creative expression through art and play provides children with an invaluable outlet for processing emotions, exploring imaginative worlds, and channeling energy in a positive way. This chapter delves into the benefits of hands-on creating and playful building for a child's development. From molding therapeutic clay figures to constructing symbolic structures, you will discover how purposeful play facilitates emotional growth, cognitive skills, eco-awareness, and more.

Children flourish when given tools to construct, deconstruct, and reconstruct their understandings of inner and outer worlds. The pages ahead offer a roadmap for this construction, inviting children on a journey limited only by imagination.

Benefits of Constructing and Sculpting in Play Therapy

Constructing and sculpting activities like molding, building, and shaping offer a wealth of benefits for a child's development. This dynamic duo enhances spatial awareness, encourages tactile exploration, and stimulates cognitive growth. Listed below are the myriad advantages these hands-on activities provide.

Building Spatial Awareness

Constructing and sculpting enhance spatial awareness—an understanding and perception of the surroundings and the relationship of objects within those surroundings.

Imagine a child attempting to fit a triangular block into a square hole or mold a ball of clay into a miniature-sized cup. These tasks require them to gauge size and shape. With time and practice, children refine their ability to discern dimensions, spatial relationships, and how different forms can interrelate.

The eyes and hands are also in tandem as children construct and sculpt. Hand-eye coordination is vital for everyday tasks, from writing to catching a ball. Children inadvertently hone this essential skill by shaping a clay figure or stacking blocks.

Encouraging Tactile Exploration

Tactile exploration, or understanding the world through touch, is fundamental in children's early developmental stages. Constructing and sculpting serve as brilliant mediums for this exploration.

From the cool, smooth sensation of clay to the grainy feel of the sand, sculpting materials offer varied tactile experiences. Engaging with these textures can be both therapeutic and educational. For instance, children initially hesitant to touch unfamiliar surfaces began exploring various materials during play therapy sessions. This tactile exploration helped them become more comfortable with diverse textures in their everyday environment.

Fine motor skills were further developed. Manipulating small objects, pinching clay, or connecting tiny pieces requires refined hand and finger movements. These detailed actions enhance a child's fine motor skills, which are essential for writing, buttoning shirts, or tying shoelaces.

Stimulating Cognitive Development

Beyond the physical, constructing and sculpting also promote cognitive growth and development.

Problem-Solving

Constructing and sculpting often involve a goal—building a tower or creating a clay figurine. Reaching that goal requires a degree of problem-solving. If a tower of blocks keeps collapsing, the child learns to reconsider its base's stability. Similarly, when a clay structure is not holding, kids reevaluate the thickness of the material used.

Imagination and Creativity

These activities are not just about following patterns or recreating models. Instead, such activities are gateways to boundless imagination. A lump of clay can transform into a fantastical creature, and a set of blocks can become a majestic castle, fostering creativity and imaginative thinking.

Persistence and Patience

Not every creation will be perfect on the first try. Constructing and sculpting teach children the value of persistence. If something does not work out, they learn the importance of trying again, tweaking their approach, and having the patience to see their vision come to life.

Emotional Clay Modeling

Clay, a pliable and yielding substance, mirrors the ever-evolving realm of human emotions. It offers a tactile, grounding medium for children to manifest their inner feelings, be they turbulent, serene, or somewhere between. Within the soft curves and edges of this earthly material, children find a language beyond words.

Smash and Rebuild

Allowing children to destroy their creations and remake something new teaches constructive coping skills for managing anger or grief. Clay smashing and rebuilding activity enables cathartic release while conveying the resilience of the human spirit. Releasing emotions through clay destruction and creating anew provides a restorative outlet with symbolic meaning. Safety emerges from trusting that we can shatter completely and still rebuild.

Objective:
- To allow healthy, contained destruction as an outlet for strong emotions.
- To process feelings about damage, loss, or change through metaphor.
- To foster hope and growth by creating something new from rubble.

Best Suited For:
This activity benefits children struggling with traumatic events, unresolved anger, or coping with loss. Ideal for ages 5 to 9 when more complex symbolism emerges.

Materials Needed:
- Air-dry or polymer clay
- Clay sculpting tools
- Surface for smashing like a cookie sheet
- Optional: tempera paint and brushes

Instructions:
1. Give your child a large lump of clay and encourage them to craft anything they want: a creature, building, pot, sculpture, etc.
2. As they mold, prompt them to think about their creation's purpose and meaning. What does it do? Why is it important? Add details that express its significance.
3. Once complete, let your child play with their finished clay piece freely, even smashing or destroying it completely! This enables safe, contained destruction.
4. While smashing, verbalize any emotions that arise—anger, disappointment, hurt, relief. Affirm all feelings are okay.
5. When ready, gently encourage them to search the rubble for surviving pieces to reuse. What remains? What can be salvaged?
6. Help them re-purpose fragments to create something new from the shards. Repeat if needed for full cathartic release.
7. When finished, have your child explain both creations—before, during, and after the destruction.

Emotion Containers

Having a physical vessel to contain difficult emotions can help children feel more in control. This activity uses clay pots symbolically decorated to represent different feelings and their triggers. Having personal clay vessels to embody difficult feelings provides a sense of containment. Decorating pots with intentional textures builds emotional understanding and regulation skills over time.

Objective:
- To promote identification and expression of emotions through creativity.
- To gain a sense of control over emotions by containing them physically.
- To clarify causes and effects related to different emotional states.

Best Suited For:
This activity benefits children who become easily overwhelmed by their feelings. It is ideal for ages 6-9 when more complex emotional understanding emerges.

Materials Needed:
- Air dry or polymer clay
- Clay sculpting tools
- Acrylic paint, markers, beads, buttons, fabric
- Emotion word list or face chart

Instructions:
1. **Provide clay and tools so your child can sculpt simple pots or jars.** Create one vessel per emotion.
2. **Refer to an emotions word list.** Choose the feelings your child struggles with most, like anger, worry, sadness, excitement, etc.
3. **Assign one emotion to represent each clay vessel.** Help them label the pots with paint, beads, etc.
4. **Look at the emotion word list together.** Have your child brainstorm possible causes or triggers for that feeling to add symbolic texture. For example:
    - *Worry Jar:* Crumpled aluminum foil to depict unpleasant thoughts.
    - *Anger Volcano:* Red paint and shakable beads for erupting.
    - *Sadness Cloud:* Weighted raindrops made from clay.
5. **Encourage them to decorate the outside of each vessel based on the feelings.** The textures should reflect what that emotion's experience is like.
6. **For containment, tiny objects that represent emotional triggers can be sealed inside.** Use foil, beads, clay pebbles, or whatever they prefer.
7. Once completed, **help your child explain the textural symbols and material meanings** they chose for each container.

Processing the Activity:
- When emotions spike, retrieve the clay container that matches what your child feels. Holding it can provide comfort and control.
- Use the vessels as symbolic props for emotional role-play and problem-solving feared triggers.

Building Emotional Structures

Children often grapple with invisible giants, fears, isolation, and fleeting moments of joy in the world of emotions. *What if these elusive feelings could take shape, weight, and form?*

Transform intangible emotions into tangible constructs, providing your child a scaffold to grasp, analyze, and ultimately navigate their intricate emotional world. Through meticulously crafted walls, islands, and jars, they confront their worries, understand their solitude, and bottle up happiness.

Wall of Worries

Physically containing worries in a symbolic block wall provides comfort and empowerment. This activity allows children to externalize anxieties and then dismantle them through play. Having a concrete visual for contained worries helps lower anxiety. Dismantling the wall piece by piece builds confidence to conquer fear before it conquers them systematically.

Objective:
- To promote identification and expression of worries in a concrete way.
- To gain a sense of control over anxiety by containing it physically.
- To practice overcoming worries through symbolic demolition.

Best Suited For:
This activity benefits anxious children who feel overwhelmed by fears and intrusive thoughts. Ideal for ages 5 to 8.

Materials Needed:
- Building blocks, Lego bricks, or wooden blocks
- Toy figures for role play, like superheroes
- Paper and crayons for labeling blocks *(optional)*

Instructions:
1. Invite your child to build a sturdy wall with blocks. Explain each block can represent a worry, fear, or concern they feel.
2. Have them hold a worry in mind and place a corresponding block down, repeating until the wall contains all current anxieties.
3. Prompt them to consider common worries like health, school, friends, family, and their future if needed. Place a block for each.
4. Once built, let your child use toy figures like superheroes to role-play conquering the Worry Wall. Knocking down each block releases that fear.
5. As they demolish blocks, empathize with each worry voiced while highlighting strengths and supports. Offer realistic reassurance.
6. Eventually, the wall will be fully dismantled. Celebrate the liberating feeling of overcoming anxieties through bravery and persistence.
7. Write a fear or worry on paper for added symbolism inside each block. Removing and tearing up the paper provides a further release.

Processing the Activity:
- **Use the Worry Wall method whenever anxiety builds up again.** Ritual demolition brings relief.

- **Reinforce their capability to confront fears.** Anxiety loses power when separated into manageable pieces.
- **Note any remaining blocks resistant to removal.** Extra support may be needed to address those specific persistent worries.
- **Validate feelings while instilling hope through consistent coping practice.** Fears lose intensity over time.

Island of Isolation

Building a symbolic island with blocks provides a perspective on isolation or loneliness. This activity allows children to externalize separation experiences in a tactile way while exploring reasons for isolation. Tactile building allows children to see isolation from a new perspective. Symbolic play builds an understanding of causes while reinforcing human resilience. With support, no island remains cut off forever.

Objective:
- To promote open discussion about isolation through concrete visualization.
- To gain an understanding of causes and effects related to feeling lonely.
- To foster hope and problem-solving by reconnecting the island.

Best Suited For:
This activity benefits children struggling with separation anxiety, loss, or social isolation. Great for ages 6 to 9.

Materials:
- Building blocks, Lego bricks, or wood blocks
- Blue cloth or paper to represent water
- Toy figures, toy boats or bridges, toy animals

Instructions:
1. Cover a table with a blue cloth. Explain this is the sea. Provide blocks and have your child build an island surrounded by water.
2. Ask open questions to understand their associations with the island imagery:
    - *Why is this island here alone?*
    - *What could be the reasons it's isolated?*
    - *How might it feel to be on this island, separated from everything else?*
    - *What might make the island want to reconnect?*
3. Allow them to place any toy figures, animals, or objects around the island relevant to their narrative. Validate their storyline and feelings.
4. Discuss ways to help the island, such as:
    - *Building boats to visit and offer comfort.*
    - *Constructing bridges to reconnect with land.*
    - *Sending messages in bottles for hope.*
5. Have your child demonstrate reuniting the island using toys. Celebrate as isolation gives way to closeness again.

Processing the Activity:
- If this activity brought up personal feelings of loneliness, empathize and explore possible solutions together.
- Highlight strengths and supports they have to avoid prolonged isolation.
- Reinforce that painful feelings are temporary states that you can work through together.

Jar of Joy

Life cannot always be sunshine and rainbows. A jar of joy helps kids collect happy reminders when they need an emotional boost. This recycled craft activity fosters gratitude, mindfulness, and resilience.

Objective:
- To promote gratitude by saving joyful memories in one place.
- To create a go-to coping tool for emotional regulation.
- To teach mindfulness of small daily blessings and pleasures.

Best Suited For:
This activity benefits sad, anxious, or lonely children needing regular mood lifts. Great for ages 5 to 9.

Materials Needed:
- Clean empty jar
- Notes, photos, ticket stubs, stickers, beads, glitter, pom poms
- Construction paper, markers, glue, string

Instructions:
1. Decorate the jar with colorful paper, stickers, glitter, etc., to make it cheery.
2. When your child experiences a happy moment, have them add a small related item or note about it to the jar.
3. Ideas: a funny joke, art project, flower from the park, movie stub.
4. Open the jar together when feeling low and reminisce over the joyful memories inside.

Processing:
- **Make your joy jar too.** Share ideas for simple pleasures that lift your mood.
- **Note patterns over time.** Discuss activities your child may want to do more often.
- **Reflect on how even small joys can brighten bad days.** Joy builds resilience.
- **Add to the jar regularly.** It can become a meaningful time capsule.

Creative Recycling

Sometimes, the essence of creativity often lies in seeing potential where others see waste. This section unfolds like a poetic tribute to the art of reinvention. It beckons children to view discarded items not as trash but as treasures, waiting for a new story to be sculpted from their forms. Here, a tattered piece of cardboard might blossom into a rich mosaic echoing the rhythms of nature while seemingly useless objects take on a fresh purpose, setting the stage for adventurous play. Through each recycled creation, children express artistry and forge a bond with our planet, learning the profound value of sustainability and the joy of metamorphosis.

Nature's Mosaic

Collecting and arranging nature's artful elements on reused cardboard fosters creativity with materials easily found outdoors. This eco-friendly mosaic project emphasizes how discarded items can be transformed into meaning. Appreciating salvaged nature and cardboard pieces as artistic media fosters ingenuity, patience, and eco-awareness. Rediscovering life's interconnected cycles brings peace of mind.

Objective:
- To spark imagination and appreciation for natural objects.
- To convey nature's interconnectedness and unlimited art potential.
- To build recycling skills by repurposing cardboard into art.

Best Suited For:
This activity benefits anxious children who need calming outdoor engagement. It also helps impatient kids practice mindful focus. Great for ages 4 to 8.

Materials Needed:
- Recycled cardboard pieces
- Natural items like leaves, petals, twigs, pebbles, pinecones
- Glue and tape for adhering items

Instructions:
1. Go outside together and allow your child time to explore freely. Have them gather up any natural objects that catch their eye.
2. Bring the treasures home and provide recycled cardboard panels for arranging pieces on. Harder items like twigs or rocks work better than soft flower petals.
3. Encourage thinking creatively about composition. There are no rules. Have fun grouping shapes, colors, and textures in unique ways.
4. Let your child select where to place each natural object on the cardboard. Glue or tape items down once positioned.
5. When complete, invite your child to describe the imagery and meaning of their finished mosaic. *Is it a landscape, animal, or abstract design?*
6. Display the nature mosaic proudly indoors or outdoors, surrounded by similar natural elements to highlight the child's eye for found beauty.

Processing the Activity:
- Note any insights gained about nature's interconnectedness and continual transformation.
- When anxious, suggest going outside mindfully together to gather more artful objects to calm the mind.
- Reflect on how disposed of items regained purpose when viewed through a creative lens.

Upcycling Obstacle Course

Transforming discarded items into an obstacle course encourages creativity, problem-solving, and sustainability values. Engineering an upcycled play space collaboratively builds bonds while fostering resourcefulness. This activity also teaches ingenuity and eco-awareness. Learning from failures builds resilience while making treasured memories.

Objective:
- To promote imaginative repurposing of recycled materials.
- To teach environmental awareness through valuing discarded items.
- To develop planning, designing, and building skills.

Best Suited For:
This activity benefits children who enjoy hands-on building and imaginative play. Great for ages 5 to 8.

Materials:
- Assorted recyclables, cardboard, bottles, cans, fabric scraps
- Masking tape, glue, string, scissors
- Outdoor space for the obstacle course

Instructions:
1. Gather a variety of recycled materials and set up an outdoor building area.
2. Encourage your child to look at the materials in new ways. *How could bottles become bowling pins? Fabric turn into flags?* Let their creativity guide brainstorming.
3. Collaborate on planning an upcycled obstacle course. Sketch designs first, then gather needed supplies.
4. Build individual course components like tunnels from cardboard boxes, fabric scrap hurdles, or spoon and bean bag races.

5. Add fun personal touches like street signs or cheering sections made from recyclables.
6. When complete, test the obstacle course together. Time trials or compete in a family challenge.

Processing the Activity:
- Discuss what skills were used in imagining and designing the course. *How did collaboration help?*
- Note any frustration, but highlight how mistakes lead to improvements. Reframe failures.
- Reflect on how discarded items gained renewed purpose when seen with creativity.
- Brainstorm ways to continue repurposing household recyclables into new games and play spaces.

Chapter 4
Crafts Activities

Whether through drawing, cutting, or gluing items together, creating with their hands opens the doorway to a child's heart. The crafts in this chapter offer parents and caregivers insight into a child's emotional experiences, fears, dreams, and memories. Each snipping, weaving, and brushstroke becomes an externalized piece of their inner selves. Far more than play, these creative hands-on activities foster emotional intelligence, self-awareness, resilience, and gratitude. With glue sticks, ribbons, and boundless creativity, discover new avenues to nurture their social-emotional growth one masterpiece at a time.

Benefits of Crafting

Every snip, paint stroke, and glued piece is a step toward holistic child development. Next time your child is engrossed in a craft activity, know they are doing much more than just *'playing'* –growing in ways that will serve them for a lifetime.

Here are some of its outstanding advantages, shedding light on why crafting is so much more than meets the eye.

Develops Fine Motor Skills

Fine motor skills refer to using and coordinating small muscle movements in the fingers, hands, and wrists. When a child threads a bead onto a string or carefully places a sticker onto paper, they hone these crucial skills. Fine motor skills are essential for daily activities like tying shoes, buttoning a shirt, or holding a pencil. By strengthening these muscles and improving coordination, children set themselves up for success in many practical life tasks.

Encourages Organizational Skills

Crafting often requires a certain level of planning and organization. From selecting the right materials to sequencing steps in the right order, children subconsciously learn how to organize their thoughts and actions. Organizational skills have far-reaching implications. In academics, for instance, being organized can mean the difference between easily locating homework assignments or endlessly searching for them, leading to undue stress.

Enhances Artistic Expression

Artistic expression is a potent medium for children to communicate feelings, ideas, and experiences. Through crafting, they can create tangible representations of their inner worlds, granting them an outlet for emotions they might not yet have the words for. Artistic expression is beyond producing beautiful creations; it is about emotional release, self-awareness, and understanding. Through art, children can process complex feelings, from joy and excitement to anger and sadness, in a safe and constructive manner.

Emotion Crafting

Crafting provides a valuable outlet for children to creatively explore, express, and understand their ever-changing inner emotional landscapes. Using diverse art materials and tactile mediums allows kids to gain insight into complex feelings in a developmentally engaging way. The activities in this section use crafts as tools to build emotional intelligence skills. Through symbolic containers, living metaphors, or interactive decorating, these hands-on exercises aim to increase emotional awareness.

While creative approaches differ, each craft activity engages children in identifying and managing emotions through purposeful play. Making feelings tangible in balloons, boxes, or sprouting seeds helps take the edge off vulnerability. In the process, kids gain healthy coping strategies to navigate inner emotional worlds.

Emotion Balloons

Inflating balloons with written or drawn emotions inside provides a tactile way to contain feelings literally and symbolically. This creative visualization activity builds emotional awareness and healthy processing skills by providing a symbolic tactile tool for identifying, containing, and releasing feelings.

Objective:
- To promote identification and expression of different emotions.
- To understand how it feels to hold in or release feelings.
- To foster coping strategies for managing overwhelming emotions constructively.

Best Suited For:
This activity benefits children who become easily emotionally flooded. It teaches regulation through mindful feeling identification and containment. Great for ages 5 to 8.

Materials Needed:
- Balloons
- Small slips of paper and pens or markers
- Optional: stickers, glitter, ribbon for decorating balloons

Instructions:
1. Have your child write or draw one emotion on individual paper slips: angry, joyful, worried, excited, lonely, proud, etc.

2. Place each feeling paper inside a separate deflated balloon and inflate it. Tie balloons to contain the feeling of air inside.
3. Encourage them to add decorative elements like stickers, ribbons, or glitter on the outside to reflect the emotion within each balloon. Get creative!
4. Line up all the feeling balloons and have your child walk you through each, naming the contained emotion and its corresponding decorative details.
5. Choose one or more balloons to pop and *"release"* those feelings. Observe their choices and process the experience together.
6. Keep any intact balloons in a safe place to revisit later. These hold contained feelings to continue exploring when ready.

Processing the Activity:
- Discuss how it feels to inflate and contain intense emotions. *Does air ever leak out gradually?*
- Reflect on whether it's easier to release some feelings versus others. *Why might that be?*
- Note any avoidance around popping certain emotions. More support may be needed to process these.
- When emotions feel too big, remind your child to imagine sealing them into a balloon to gain control.

Feelings Garden

Like garden plants, caring for seeds planted to represent emotions fosters an understanding of how feelings emerge and evolve. Nurturing their miniature *"feelings garden"* teaches empathy, growth mindset, and regulation skills. White having caregiving responsibilities builds attachment and pride, which transfer to emotional intelligence.

Objective:
- To build empathy for how emotions develop over time with care.
- To practice nurturing seeds metaphorically linked to feelings.
- To gain experience with the growth process both emotionally and botanically.

Best Suited For:
This activity benefits emotionally sensitive children who become easily overwhelmed. It teaches externalizing and managing feelings. Great for ages 4 to 8.

Materials Needed:
- Small pots, soil, emotive seeds like sunflowers or vines
- Popsicle sticks, straws, pipe cleaners
- Markers, foam shapes, stickers to decorate sticks
- Watering can spray bottle

Instructions:
1. Help your child fill pots with soil and plant a seed in each. Select seeds that stretch or sprout dramatically as they grow.
2. Assign an emotion representing each pot, like joy, anger, or fear. Use decorated sticks to mark the feeling.
3. Explain that the seeds will grow with consistent care, like feelings growing stronger in response to attention.
4. Set up a window garden space and encourage your child to check on the pots daily, expressing and tending to the represented emotions.
5. Each day, prompt discussions using gardening as an emotional metaphor while they care for the plants.
    - *Do some feelings need more nurturing to grow than others? Why might that be?*

- *What helps big feelings shrink down to size so they do not overwhelm us?*
6. Continue comparing the seedlings' physical growth to emotional development until fully sprouted.

Processing the Activity:
- Reflect on insights gained regarding emotional change over time. Feelings are constantly evolving.
- Note which emotion plants thrived most with care. *Do certain feelings come easier to your child?*
- Use the feelings garden concept when children become upset. Suggest picturing that emotion as a seedling they can nurture or neglect.

Vision Boards

In a child's imagination, dreams blossom and take flight, free from the constraints of reality. Vision boards are a captivating avenue for these young minds to map out their desires, hopes, and dreams in vibrant color and detail. Think of them as a treasure map, with each image, sticker, or drawing symbolizing a beacon of what they wish for, aspire to, or hope to become. Just as navigators once used stars to guide their way, children can use these vision boards to chart a course for their dreams, providing both a playful activity and a powerful tool for introspection and goal setting.

Dream Haven

Every kid has imagined their dream home at some point. Whether it's a castle with a dragon-guarded tower, a cozy cottage in the woods, or a space-age house on Mars, these dreams provide a fascinating window into a child's aspirations, personality, and the comfort they seek. This activity invites children to craft their vision of a future home, providing insights into what they value, desire, and dream of. It also serves as a therapeutic tool to explore a child's feelings, desires, and understanding of comfort and security.

Objective:
- To empower children to envision and express their aspirations for the future.
- To stimulate creativity, planning, and spatial thinking.
- To understand a child's perception of safety, comfort, and happiness.

Best Suited For:
Particularly beneficial for children who have recently experienced a change in their living situation, like moving homes, or have expressed curiosity about different places and ways of living. Ideally crafted for ages 4 to 9.

Materials Needed:
- Posterboard
- House & interior magazine cutouts
- Markers in various colors
- Stickers *(preferably with home and nature themes)*
- Glue

Instructions:
1. **Discuss the concept of a home.** Address questions like, *"What makes a house a home?", "Why is it essential?"* and *"How do different people live worldwide?".* Such questions establish the foundation for the activity.
2. **Provide them with the poster board and introduce it as the canvas for their dream home.** Posterboards are where they get to design everything they have ever wanted in a house. The only limit is their imagination.
3. **Let them go through the magazine cutouts, identifying items or spaces they'd love to incorporate.** *Is there*

a grand staircase they fancy? Or a room filled with aquarium walls? Let them cut these out and set them aside.

4. **With markers, guide them to sketch the outline of their home.** It could be a multi-story mansion or a single-story beachside house. Allow their creativity to flow.
5. **Once the outline is established, place the magazine cutouts on the poster board, deciding where each room or feature goes.** Encourage them to draw, color, and decorate further, filling in areas not covered by the magazine images.
6. **Stickers can be used to add additional features or decorative elements.** *Maybe a garden with mythical creatures? Or a treehouse linked to the main home by a swing?*
7. **As they craft, engage them in conversation about their choices.** *Why did they choose a specific feature? What does it mean to them?*
8. **Once their dream home is complete, hang it up in a space where they can see it daily.** It serves as a beautiful reminder of their aspirations and the safety of the home they envision.

Processing the Activity:
- **Engage in a reflective discussion about their dream haven.** *What were the most essential features for them?* Often, your kid's choices provide insights into what they currently cherish or perhaps miss.
- **Discuss the feelings associated with home.** If they have added unique safety features or protective elements, delve deeper to understand any underlying fears or anxieties.
- **Celebrate their creativity.** Every child's dream haven will be different, and that is the beauty of it. It directly reflects their unique personality, aspirations, and feelings.
- **Reiterate that while this is a dream home, the most vital aspect of any home is the love, warmth, and

safety it offers. It is not about the size or luxury but the emotions and memories created within its walls.

Heart's Canvas

The heart is like a canvas, bearing imprints of everything you love and cherish. These joys, no matter how big or small, shape your daily lives and fill your world with color and happiness. The activity invites children to visually express all they hold dear, helping them recognize and celebrate their various sources of joy. Through this, children not only get a creative outlet but also embark on a journey of self-reflection. It is a therapeutic tool to boost their mood, reinforce gratitude, and emphasize the significance of cherishing the things they love.

Objective:
- To provide children an avenue to recognize and articulate things they love.
- To foster gratitude by acknowledging the joys in their life.
- To reinforce the importance of cherishing happy memories and moments.

Best Suited For:
Particularly beneficial for children who might be going through phases where they are feeling low or have had recent experiences that overshadow their usual joys. It serves as a reminder of all the love and happiness around them. Perfect for ages 3 to 9.

Materials Needed:
- Cardboard *(preferably large enough for a collage)*
- Paints in various colors
- Brushes of different sizes
- Magazine cutouts
- Glue

Instructions:
1. Discuss what it means to love something. *Is it only about big things, or can small moments and things also bring joy?* Doing so will help your child understand that significant events and everyday moments can be sources of happiness.
2. Give the cardboard and explain that it is where they get to paint, stick, and showcase everything they love.
3. Let them paint a background on the cardboard. Instruct them to choose a color that they feel represents love or joy. Allow them to take their time, ensuring it is an expressive process rather than just a step to get done.
4. Hand over the magazine cutouts or have pictures printed out. They can look for images that resonate with things they love. It could be a picture of a pet, a type of food, a hobby, or even a favorite place.
5. Once they have selected their images, glue them onto the painted cardboard. They can also paint or draw directly onto the board to depict something specific.
6. Encourage them to tell a story through their canvas. *Why did they choose certain images? How do they feel when they think about these things?*
7. Once the heart's canvas is complete, find a special place to hang or display it. This way, your child is reminded daily of everything they love, especially when they might feel down or overwhelmed.

Processing the Activity:
- **Engage your child in a conversation about their heart's canvas.** Discuss the choices they made and the feelings associated with each element.
- **Highlight the importance of gratitude.** Recognize and be thankful for all the love and joy in their life, no matter how small.
- **Talk about the feelings of happiness and comfort that the canvas brings.** On challenging days, they can

look at their canvas and be reminded of everything that brings them joy.
- **Reiterate the idea that love and joy come from various sources.** Whether it is a favorite toy, a beloved family member, or even a cherished memory, every bit of happiness contributes to their well-being.

Memory and Experience Crafts

As the river of time flows steadily, it carries myriad memories and experiences, each shaping the story of our lives. Through the activities below, children are offered a sanctuary to pause, to dip into this river, and to draw out the golden moments that have touched their souls. These crafts are not just simple activities as they are windows into a child's past, reflecting their friendships, identities, and cherished moments.

Bonds on Board

Friendships are the vibrant threads that add color, texture, and warmth to life. These bonds, forged in shared experiences and mutual affection, form the cornerstone of our social development and emotional well-being. The *"Bonds on Board"* activity enables children to visually honor these relationships, allowing them to recognize the significance of friendships and the joy they bring into their lives.

Objective:
- To provide children with an avenue to acknowledge and celebrate their friendships.
- To strengthen their understanding of relationships, mutual respect, and shared experiences.
- To boost their self-esteem and sense of belonging by recognizing the bonds they've formed.

Best Suited For:
Particularly fruitful for children learning the value of friendships, those who might feel isolated or have recently experienced changes in their social circles, such as moving to a new school. A heartwarming exercise for ages 3 to 9, reminding them of their cherished companions.

Materials Needed:
- Posterboard
- Photos of friends *(printed or hand-drawn)*
- Stickers with themes of friendship, fun, and unity
- Ribbons in various colors
- Markers in multiple shades

Instructions:
1. Begin with a conversation about friendships. Discuss questions like, *"What makes someone a good friend?", "How do friends make us feel?"* and *"What fun things do you like to do with your friends?".* Doing so primes them for the activity, helping them reflect on their relationships.
2. Explain that this activity will celebrate and honor their friends. The poster board will bring together memories, shared moments, and everything that symbolizes their friendships.
3. Invite them to place photos or drawings of their friends on the board. These images serve as the primary focus, the anchors of their vision board.
4. With markers, tell your child to write names, draw doodles, or even jot down memories associated with each friend. Maybe there is an inside joke they want to record or a special day they wish to remember.
5. Use stickers to embellish the space around each photo. These can symbolize activities they love together, like playing at a park, reading stories, or sharing hobbies.

6. The ribbons come into play next. Intertwined the ribbon, forming links between photos, symbolizing the interconnectedness of their friendships. The myriad colors can signify the diverse emotions and experiences each friend brings into their life.
7. As the board takes shape, it becomes more than just a collection of photos and decorations. It becomes a vivid representation of their social world, brimming with memories, laughter, and shared moments.

Processing the Activity:
- **Engage in a discussion about the completed "Bonds on Board."** Dive into the stories behind each photo, each sticker, and each ribbon. This allows you to understand their social dynamics and reinforces their memories.
- **Highlight the importance of cherishing friendships.** Old and new friends shape lives, offering companionship, support, and endless moments of joy.
- **When the child feels isolated or left out, the board serves as a tangible reminder of their social connections.** It can be a tool to boost their morale and confidence.
- **Reiterate the value of mutual respect, understanding, and compassion in friendships.** These bonds are built on trust, and nurturing them with care, kindness, and love is essential.

Time Capsule

Creating a personalized time capsule allows children to gather mementos and preserve present-day memories. Filling a container with objects representing their current self fosters self-reflection. The stored artifacts become sentimental keepsakes for rediscovering their past selves years later. Compiling personal time capsules allows children to cherish who they are in the present while eagerly anticipating who they will become. Looking back connects us to ourselves through time.

Objective:
- To promote introspection and gratitude through collecting meaningful memorabilia.
- To gain perspective on how personal identities and priorities evolve.
- To build anticipation for rediscovering preserved memories and revisiting the past.

Best Suited For:
This activity is ideal during transitional life stages like moving homes, starting school, or welcoming a new sibling. Great for ages 5 to 9.

Materials Needed:
- Small sealed box or container
- Paper, pens, markers, stickers, photos
- Trinkets to represent interests like art, trophies
- Optional: duct tape, glue, plastic wrap to seal

Instructions:
1. Provide your child with a container to decorate however they wish. Explain this will become their special time capsule.
2. Have them gather items and create notes that represent who they are, what they love, and what they want to remember right now in their life.
3. Let them decide what safe keepsakes to include, such as favorite toys, drawings, schoolwork, photos, letters, and memorabilia.
4. Guide them to include reflective elements like predictions, goals, and advice to their future selves.

5. When their time capsule feels complete, help them seal it securely with tape, glue, and plastic wrap.
6. Conduct a *"burying"* ceremony in the backyard as a family, and note the date you will reopen it years later.
7. On the chosen future date, dig up and unseal the capsule together. Reminisce over its contents, reflecting on memories, growth, and predictions.

Processing the Activity:
- Revisit the time capsule occasionally before the future opening date. Add items yearly.
- When coping with change, relate the contents to what used to be important and familiar.
- Note interests and priorities that evolved versus those that remain unchanged.
- Discuss the emotions that emerge when rediscovering meaningful memorabilia.

Memory Magnets

Creating miniature artwork or photo magnets gives children a keepsake for displaying cherished memories on the refrigerator. Having happy snapshots and art within view promotes positive reminiscence and family bonding.

Objective:
- To promote gratitude and positive reflection through choosing meaningful memories to preserve.
- To build narrative skills by recounting stories behind chosen moments.
- To foster family connection and identity with displayed memories.

Best Suited For:
This activity is ideal for grieving or changing families to honor past joyful times. It also benefits children with memory challenges. Great for ages 4 to 8.

Materials Needed:
- Sturdy cardboard, card stock, or thick paper
- Childhood photos, magazine clippings
- Glue sticks, scissors, hole punch
- Markers, crayons, art stickers
- Small round magnets

Instructions:
1. Cut the cardboard into small uniform pieces for your child to decorate as mini memory boards.
2. Have them illustrate a meaningful memory on each board. Alternatively, glue a photo or magazine picture representing a shared family experience.
3. Ask them to describe the special memory as they decorate. *What happened? Why was it meaningful?* Details are key.
4. Help attach a magnet to the back of each finished memory board. Punch a hole first for durability.
5. Display the magnetic memories together on the refrigerator to revisit and reminisce over daily.

Processing the Activity:
- When separating from your child, encourage bringing a couple of magnets for comfort.
- Note any memories your child avoids depicting. These may signal needed conversations.
- Add new memory magnets regularly to chronicle your family's story over time.
- Rotate old memories to a memory book sometimes to make space for new ones.
- Create special shared memory magnets to model reminiscing and highlighting positive times.

Chapter 5
Dancing and Music Activities

From ancient rituals to modern-day celebrations, dancing and music have been integral to human expression across cultures. This chapter delves into the wonderful benefits that dancing and music can provide, especially within the context of play therapy for children. Through diverse activities, you will explore how movement and sound can become channels for building skills, processing emotions, and unlocking creative potential.

Benefits of Dancing and Music

More than just a form of entertainment, dancing and music bring a plethora of benefits that can be especially impactful in play therapy, such as:

Develop Motor Skills

When you think of dancing, many imagine gracefully coordinated movements. Dancing, structured or freestyle, helps improve balance, agility, and coordination. For instance, a simple activity like dancing to the tune of *"The Hokey Pokey"* not only introduces children to different parts of their body but also helps them coordinate their movements to match the song's instructions.

Build Muscle Memory Through Repetition

The repetitive nature of certain dance steps or routines ensures that participants build muscle memory. This repetition is like how a child might practice riding a bicycle or tying their shoes until the skill becomes second nature. As they practice their dance moves, children become more aware of their bodies, understanding how each part moves with the others.

Encourage Emotional Release

Music and dancing provide a safe and constructive outlet for emotions. When your child feels joy, sadness, or frustration, dancing can help them express these feelings without needing words. For example, a child feeling overwhelmed could find solace in moving to the calming tunes of a lullaby.

Children can also learn to navigate the emotional landscape by engaging in dance and music activities. It allows them to experience various feelings in a controlled environment, understanding that feeling and expressing emotions is natural.

Stimulate Auditory and Rhythmic Skills

Even babies can be seen bobbing their heads or swaying to a beat. Such an innate response to music demonstrates the human brain's natural affinity for rhythm. Through dancing and listening to music, children can enhance their auditory skills, learning to differentiate between various beats, tempos, and melodies.

Expressive Dance

Dance is a language that speaks from the soul, using the body as its canvas to paint stories, emotions, and ideas. For young minds, dancing is an exploration—a playful interaction between space, sound, and self. From casting enchanting shadows that tell tales of imagination to mirroring a partner's every move in a harmonious dance of connection, these activities introduce children to the joys of expressive movement. Not only do they foster physical awareness and creativity, but they also offer invaluable lessons in focus, coordination, and the ebbs and flows of relationships.

Shadow Dance

Dancing to cast imaginative shadows on the wall fosters body awareness, problem-solving, and creative thinking. Manipulating light and movement to design shadow shapes and stories helps children gain a new perspective.

Objective:
- To build spatial body awareness and coordination through interactive shadow play.
- To spark imagination and storytelling by inventing shadow shapes and scenarios.
- To gain insight into alternate perspectives by looking at light and shadows in new ways.

Best Suited For:
This activity benefits children who have a restless energy and need active engagement. It also helps shy kids come out of their shell. Great for ages 4 to 8.

Materials Needed:
- Flashlight, lamp, or overhead projector
- Blank wall space to cast shadows
- Upbeat music *(optional)*

Instructions:
1. Cast a strong, focused light on a blank wall to create defined shadows. Dim other lights.

2. Encourage your child to make shapes with their hands and body between the light and wall. *What do their shadows resemble? Can they create a dog or bird shape?*
3. Play fun shadow-guessing games. Take turns forming silhouettes and having the other person identify the shadowed object.
4. Next, prompt them to move their body to tell a story with shadow motions. Add music to Dance their shadow story like a puppet show.
5. Let their imagination run wild, combining movements and hand shapes to design new shadow creatures, people, and actions.
6. Finally, switch roles allow them to cast shadows for you to dance with. Mimic each other's shadow shapes.

Processing the Activity:
- Discuss the experience of seeing themselves in a new shadow form. *Did it change their body perceptions?*
- Reflect on how adjusting angles and distances transformed their shadows. Different perspectives create new outlooks.
- When emotions are big, suggest visualizing them as changeable shadows rather than permanent states.
- Make it a nightly ritual or any time boredom strikes! Shadow play promotes creativity.

Mirror Dance

Mirroring a dance partner's movements helps children build focus, coordination, and teamwork skills. Taking turns leading and following teaches the give-and-take of relationships. Moving in sync, partners must closely observe each other's cues.

Objective:
- To develop body awareness, control, and visual tracking skills.
- To practice mindful focus, listening, and cooperation through movement.
- To foster confidence and leadership skills when taking turns guiding the dance.

Best Suited For:
This activity benefits children who need to improve focus or social skills with peers. It encourages shy kids to take the lead. Great for ages 4 to 8.

Materials Needed:
- Upbeat instrumental music
- Open space free of obstacles

Instructions:
1. Face your child and explain one partner will start as the leader, making slow dance moves for the other to mirror them.
2. As a leader, demonstrate fun, simple movements like gracefully stepping from side to side, twisting, and sweeping arms. Invite them to precisely imitate each move.
3. Praise their efforts to observe and match their body to your motions carefully.
4. After a short time, they swap roles to become the dance leaders. Remind them to start with slow, repetitive moves that are easy to follow.
5. When ready, incorporate more complex sequences, emotions, or stories for the mirroring partner to interpret through movement.
6. Allow several turns leading and mirroring. Provide supportive feedback and dynamism.

Processing the Activity:
- Discuss what skills they had to use, like focus, patience, teamwork, and communication.
- Reflect on how it felt to lead versus mirror the partner. *Which did they prefer?*
- Ask how accurately they observed body language and emotions conveyed through dance.
- Practice regularly to build observational abilities and movement confidence.

Freeze Dance

Dancing freely and abruptly freezing builds listening skills, body awareness, and self-control. This lively stop-and-go game requires focus and agility. Taking fun musical breaks for freeze dancing teaches children to manage their energy constructively.

Objective:
- To improve auditory attention skills and response inhibition through active listening games.
- To build awareness and control over one's body and impulses.
- To establish healthy outlets for energetic expression.

Best Suited For:
This activity benefits children who have difficulty with self-regulation and impulse control. It also motivates quiet kids. Great for ages 4 to 8.

Materials Needed:
- Upbeat music with defined stops and starts
- Open space free of obstacles

Instructions:
1. Explain when the music starts that they can dance expressively however they want. But when it stops, they must freeze immediately.
2. Start the music, allowing them to move energetically. Let them be silly – the goal is playful expression.
3. Stop the song abruptly after a minute. Remind them to freeze completely and hold their pose.
4. Once frozen, encourage them to pay close attention to their body placement and muscle tension. *What do they feel?*
5. After several seconds, restart the music and praise successful freezing. Repeat stop-and-go cycles regularly.
6. To up the challenge, announce freeze cues randomly instead of waiting for song stops. Increase the freeze duration.

Processing the Activity:
- Discuss what skills they had to use, like listening, waiting, and staying focused.
- Reflect on how relaxing or difficult it felt to go from dancing to total stillness.
- Incorporate as brain breaks when emotions or energy escalate. Suggest a freeze dance to reset and refocus.
- Make it a ritual for energizing mornings or calming bedtime routines. Freeze dancing balances vitality.

Rhythmic Emotions

Rhythms pulse within us, a constant dance of the heart that resonates with our deepest emotions and states of being. The magic of rhythmic emotions lies in their universal language—a language that bridges the gap between mind and body, thought and sensation. It is a world where heartbeats tell tales of inner feelings, and music catalyzes profound emotional journeys.

Heartbeat Listening

Tuning into the body's natural heartbeat rhythm helps children understand how emotions create physical responses. Listening to their pulse at rest and after activity builds mind-body awareness. Heart rates reflect the inner states.

Objective:
- To develop mindful focus and listening skills by tuning into the body's rhythmic patterns.
- To gain insight into how the heart responds to different mental and emotional states.
- To establish tools for self-regulation through purposeful breathing.

Best Suited For:
This activity benefits anxious children who need concrete calming skills. It also helps energetic kids practice stillness. Great for ages 5 to 8.

Materials Needed:
- Timer
- Calm music *(optional)*
- Stuffed animal or toy to represent the heartbeat

Instructions:
1. After physical activity, have your child sit quietly and place their hand over their heart. Set a timer for 1 minute.
2. Ask them to focus closely on the throbbing sensations under their hand to tune into their heartbeat. Have them describe how it feels – *fast? Strong? Steady?*
3. When the timer ends, explain how heart rates reflect mood and energy level. Faster pulses match feelings of excitement or anxiety.

4. Play soft music and have them re-listen to their heartbeat. Time 1 minute again.
5. Discuss how the rhythm changes. Ask what makes it slow down or speed up. Guide them to take a few deep breaths while listening.
6. Let them mime a slower heartbeat with a stuffed animal on their chest, rising and falling.

Processing the Activity:
- When worried, remind them to listen to their heartbeat and take calming, deep breaths.
- Note how emotions create physical responses, but we can also use physical cues to change feelings.
- Make listening to heartbeats a regular mindfulness practice during noisy or energetic times. Internal rhythms instill calm.

Emotion Dance Tags

Dancing out different emotions to matching musical rhythms helps children advance their emotional vocabulary and body awareness. Taking turns leading as *"taggers"* enables safe emotional expression and role play. Moving minds and bodies together builds bonds.

Objective:
- To expand the ability to identify emotions and associated body language.
- To practice expressing feelings through improvised dance movements.
- To build confidence and empathy by leading as taggers who set the emotion.

Best Suited For:
This activity benefits children who struggle to label emotions or lack opportunities for creative physical outlets. Great for ages 4 to 8.

Materials Needed:
- Upbeat instrumental music with variable tempos
- Open space free of obstacles
- List of emotions written out

Instructions:
1. Select an emotion and play a matching song rhythm: fast for joy, slow for sadness. Demonstrate dancing accordingly.
2. Encourage your child to dance the emotion with you, feeling the beat and moving expressively.
3. Take turns calling out emotions while changing the music to match. Perform dance interpretations together.
4. Add props like scarves to extend the dance and storytelling. *How might a scared dance move compared to an angry or silly one?*
5. Guide your child when needed in conveying emotions accurately through tempo and body language.
6. Switch leadership roles allow your child to pick songs and initiate emotive dance tags. Provide praise for creativity.

Processing the Activity:
- Discuss which emotions were easiest to express through movement. *Which proved more difficult?*
- Reflect on how the tagger role felt compared to the follower. *Did one build more confidence?*
- When conflicts arise, re-enact the situation through emotional dance. Resolve it with a collaborative dance.

Emotion Soundtrack

Music has the incredible ability to evoke emotions and memories. Within its beats, melodies, and rhythms, children can discover a platform to express their deepest feelings. The *'Emotion Soundtrack'* activity is designed to help children tap into their feelings using the language of music.

Objective:
- To encourage children to explore, identify, and express their emotions.
- To create an auditory representation of their feelings.
- To develop collaboration skills and respect for others' feelings.

Best Suited For:
This activity is ideal for children aged 4 to 9 who may struggle to articulate their emotions through words. It aids in verbal and non-verbal emotional expression and is also suitable for those looking to foster team-building skills.

Materials Needed:
- Various simple instruments like tambourines, maracas, toy drums, triangles, xylophones.
- A device to record the music *(optional)*.
- Sheets of paper and colored markers or crayons for drawing.
- Comfortable seating arrangements in a circle.

Instructions:
1. Begin with a brief discussion about emotions, asking questions such as:
    - *How do you feel when it rains?*
    - *What about when someone gives you a surprise?*

2. Then, connect these feelings to sounds. For instance, the rhythm of rain might be represented by the gentle tapping of a drum.
3. Introduce each instrument, one at a time, showcasing how it sounds. Discuss the feelings each sound might evoke. For instance, a fast shake of a maraca might sound like excitement, while a slow one might sound like calm waves by the beach.
4. Have each child pick an emotion they would like to express. They could even draw an emoticon face representing their emotion.
5. Allow the children to pick an instrument that best matches their chosen emotion. Encourage them to explore the instrument, figuring out how to manipulate it to produce the sound that aligns with their feelings.
6. Once each child has chosen their emotion and instrument, gather them in a circle. Explain that they'll be creating an "Emotion Soundtrack" together. Each child will get a chance to play their instrument, expressing their emotion, while the others listen.
7. Using a recording device, record each child's contribution to the soundtrack. This gives them a tangible representation of their feelings and serves as a precious memory.
8. Once the soundtrack is complete, have a sharing session. Ask questions like:
    - *How did it feel to express your emotion through music?*
    - *Was it easier or more challenging than saying how you felt?*
    - *How did it feel listening to others' emotions?*

Processing the Activity:
- **Discuss the various emotions expressed during the activity.** Recognizing and naming emotions is the first step toward understanding and managing them.
- **Reflect on the collaborative aspect of the activity.** *Which emotions were similar? Which were different? How did it feel to create something collectively?*

- **Talk about the importance of expressing emotions and how music is just one of many outlets.** Encourage your child to use their *"Emotion Soundtrack"* as a reference in the future, reminding them of the feelings they've explored.
- **Highlight the connection between emotions and music.** Discuss how different tunes or songs they hear daily might make them feel and why.

Explorative Singing

The voice becomes a powerful instrument of expression, echoing the heart's deepest sentiments. Explorative singing is a journey where the soul finds solace in melodies, harmonies, and lyrics. Whether the exuberant energy of karaoke, the soothing hum that resonates with your core, or the poetic allure of crafting a song, singing invites children to traverse an enchanting soundscape where feelings come alive.

Emotion Karaoke

Music has a magical quality: it speaks to our souls, often helping to articulate emotions we might struggle to express otherwise. Karaoke, a beloved activity by many, allows individuals to step into the shoes of their favorite artists and sing their hearts out. *"Emotion Karaoke"* integrates the therapeutic aspects of music with the joy of singing, enabling children to voice their feelings in a fun and engaging manner.

Objective:
- To enable children to identify and express emotions through song lyrics.
- To foster a sense of confidence in vocalizing feelings.
- To enhance social skills through group participation and support.

Best Suited For:
Children between the ages of 4 to 9, especially those who might struggle to articulate their emotions verbally. This activity is particularly beneficial for enhancing self-expression, building self-esteem, and promoting social interaction.

Materials Needed:
- Karaoke machine or a device with speaker capabilities *(like a computer or tablet)*.
- A selection of child-appropriate songs with varying emotional themes *(happiness, sadness, bravery, etc.)*
- Microphones *(if available, but not mandatory)*.
- Lyric sheets for each selected song.
- Comfortable seating and a *"stage"* area.

Instructions:
1. Begin by discussing different emotions with the child. Talk about times they felt happy, sad, excited, or scared. Relate these feelings to different situations or events in their life.
2. Introduce the idea of karaoke. Explain that songs often tell stories or express feelings and that today, they will pick songs that resonate with their feelings.
3. Play short snippets of the pre-selected songs. After each snippet, discuss the emotions conveyed in the song. For instance, after playing a cheerful song, you could discuss how it made the child feel and what happy events it might remind them of.
4. Allow the child to choose a song that they resonate with emotionally. Hand them the lyric sheet and let them familiarize themselves with the words.
5. Once they are ready, set the stage for their performance! Dim the lights if possible, give them the microphone, and play the song's karaoke version.

6. As the child sings, observe their emotional expression. Note if they seem more connected to certain lines or if their mood shifts with the song.
7. After their performance, applaud their efforts. Discuss how it felt to sing out their feelings. Was it liberating? Fun? Challenging?
8. If multiple children are participating, turn it into a supportive group activity. After each child's performance, encourage the others to talk about how the song made them feel, promoting empathy and understanding.
9. Conclude the session by reflecting on the power of music. Discuss how, just like karaoke, they can always turn to songs to help them understand and express their emotions daily.

Processing the Activity:
- After the activity, build on the emotions expressed in the songs. Create a list of new emotional words that they learned or felt during the activity.
- Relate the themes of the songs to events in the child's life. For instance, if a song talks about friendship, discuss their friends and related feelings.

Humming and Healing

Sound, in its various forms, can resonate with the innermost feelings. Among these sounds, humming holds a unique space. The soft, continuous notes produced while humming can have a therapeutic impact on our well-being. Through the *"Humming and Healing"* activity, your children can explore the calming and harmonious effects of humming, creating an auditory sanctuary that can help process emotions and foster tranquility.

Objective:
- To introduce children to the therapeutic benefits of humming.
- To enable emotional self-regulation through simple vocal exercises.
- To create a personal calming routine that can be accessed during emotional turbulence.

Best Suited For:
Children aged 4 to 9, especially those who might be experiencing anxiety, stress, or emotional disturbances. This activity offers a gentle method for self-soothing and is adaptable for individual and group settings.

Materials Needed:
- A comfortable and quiet space for relaxation.
- Gentle background music or nature sounds *(optional)*.
- Soft cushions or mats for sitting or lying down.

Instructions:
1. Begin by creating a serene environment, dimming the lights, and arranging soft cushions or mats in a circle. Start using background music at a low volume, ensuring it doesn't overpower the child's humming.
2. Discuss the concept of humming. You can mention how sometimes, when people are happy, thoughtful, or even anxious, they might hum a tune without even realizing it.
3. Encourage the child to take a few deep breaths, inhaling through the nose and exhaling through the mouth. As they become more relaxed, ask them to start humming during the exhale.
4. Introduce the idea of humming different 'feelings.' For instance, *what does a happy hum sound like? How about a curious hum or a calm hum?* Allow them to experiment with different pitches and durations of humming.

5. If multiple children are participating, turn it into a collective activity. Start a humming chain, where one child begins and, after a few moments, the next child joins in, creating a harmonious blend of hums.
6. Incorporate body movements. As they hum, they can sway gently, allowing the vibrations from their humming to resonate throughout their body.
7. Once the humming session feels complete, ask them to soften their hums until they transition into silence gradually. Allow a few moments of quiet reflection.
8. Discuss the experience. *How did it feel to fill the room with their hums? Did they feel the vibrations?* Were there moments when they felt particularly connected to a certain emotion?

Processing the Activity:
- Invite your child to reflect on the sensory aspect of the activity. *How did the vibrations feel? Did they notice any calming effects or changes in their body, like a slower heartbeat or relaxed muscles?*
- Encourage your child to incorporate humming into their daily routine, especially during moments of distress. Highlight that this activity can be a tool for them, a personal sanctuary they can access whenever they need a moment of calm.

Songwriting Therapy

While some emotions can be easily communicated through words, others might need a different channel. Music, with its melodies and rhythms, offers such a channel to release emotions. The *'Songwriting Therapy'* activity offers your children a platform to weave their feelings into songs, offering them an outlet for expression and a keepsake of their emotional journey.

Objective:
- To allow children to articulate and process their emotions by creating personalized songs.
- To stimulate creativity and boost self-confidence by crafting their lyrics and melodies.
- To provide a therapeutic outlet where emotions transform into art.

Best Suited For:
Designed especially for children aged 4 to 9 who possess a vivid imagination and are keen to explore diverse ways of expressing themselves. Particularly beneficial for those who might be going through emotional upheavals and need a constructive outlet to channel their feelings.

Materials Needed:
- Blank sheets of paper or a notebook for jotting down lyrics.
- Colored pens or pencils for writing.
- A simple musical instrument like a keyboard, guitar, or a music-playing device to play popular tunes.
- Recording device *(optional)* to capture the original songs.

Instructions:
1. Introduce the world of songwriting. Highlight that songs are stories or messages set to melodies. They can be about anything—a beautiful day, a lost toy, or feelings like happiness, sadness, or excitement.
2. Encourage your child to think of a theme or emotion they want to sing about. It could be a recent event, an upcoming birthday, or feelings about a friend.
3. Provide them with the materials and allow them to draft their lyrics on paper. Remind them there is no right or wrong here. Express what they feel.

4. Once they have their lyrics, introduce the concept of a tune or melody. If they are familiar with a musical instrument, they can try setting their lyrics to a tune of their creation. Alternatively, they can use the tune of a well-known children's song and adapt their lyrics to fit.
5. As they work on their song, be present to guide, encourage, and support. Offer praises for their creativity and provide gentle feedback when necessary.
6. When they are ready, create a mini *"concert"* environment. Allow them to perform their original song. If there are multiple participants, this can become a sharing session, allowing children to listen, appreciate, and understand each other's feelings through their songs.
7. If possible, record their performance. This gives them a sense of accomplishment and serves as a memento to reflect upon later.
8. Discuss the emotions encapsulated in their song. Delve deeper into the lyrics, trying to understand the feelings and stories behind them. Doing so allows them to open up about any bottled-up emotions or experiences.

Processing the Activity:
- After the songwriting session, spend time with your child discussing the feelings they sang about. *How did it feel to translate emotions into words and music? Was it liberating or challenging?*
- Reflect on the creative process. *How did they feel crafting a song from scratch? Did they discover any new talents or interests in the process?*
- Play back the recorded song, if available. Discuss the emotions it evokes now. Sometimes, listening to their creation gives children a fresh perspective on their feelings.
- Encourage the child to use songwriting as a future tool whenever they feel overwhelmed with emotions. It can be their outlet, providing solace and understanding.

Chapter 6
Acting and Storytelling Activities

As young minds engage in make-believe through acting and storytelling, their imagination comes alive. Whether narrating tales with hand puppets or role-playing family dynamics, such activities tap into a child's natural affinity for pretend play. More profoundly, they provide a medium to safely explore emotions, build empathy and communication skills, and strengthen relationships.

In this chapter, journey into acting and storytelling as pathways for growth and healing. Through engaging exercises and reflective discussions, your children can step into new roles, give voice to puppets, and weave personal tales. As emerging emotions are expressed, stories unfold, and performances come center stage, the true magic happens.

Benefits of Acting and Storytelling

You may wonder, *"Why should I consider introducing acting and storytelling activities to my child?"* Using dolls to enact a scenario or narrating a short, imaginative tale, the world of acting and storytelling offers various benefits, some of which are stated below.

Building Empathy and Understanding

Imagine your child playing the role of a sad puppy or a lonely tree. As they immerse themselves in these characters, they are essentially walking in the *"shoes"* of another being, enabling children to understand and feel emotions from another perspective. For instance, after playing the role of a bullied character, your child might realize how painful bullying can be, leading them to be more inclusive and kinder in real life.

Consider classic tales like *"The Ugly Duckling"* or *"Cinderella."* These stories reflect deeper emotional experiences. As children hear and relate to these stories, they can recognize feelings of loneliness, longing, or hope in the characters, mirroring their own emotions. Recognizing emotions in characters helps children acknowledge and process their feelings, building a deeper understanding of themselves and others.

Encouraging Verbal Expression

Sometimes, children find it hard to express their feelings directly. Acting offers them an indirect channel. By adopting a character, they can voice feelings or problems that they might find too challenging to discuss as themselves. For example, a child might use a teddy bear to say, *"Teddy is scared of the dark."* While it appears the teddy is speaking, the child communicates their fear in a safe and indirect manner.

Storytelling also offers a medium for verbal expression. Children learn to associate words with emotions by listening to or creating stories. When a character in a story feels *'angry'* or *'happy,'* children can recognize and name those emotions, equipping them with a vocabulary to express their feelings.

Enhancing Memory and Recall

Remember how you could easily recall the tales your grandparents told you but struggled with your history lessons? Stories, especially when enacted, make for memorable experiences. When children act out scenes or stories, they physically engage with the narrative, making it easier to remember.

Suppose your child learns about sharing through a story where animals in the forest learn to share food. If they enact this story, playing the role of different animals, they will likely remember the lesson about sharing even better.

Humans are biologically wired to remember stories. Our ancestors used tales to pass down vital information. Today, when a child listens to a story, their brain naturally seeks a pattern and meaning, making it easier to recall. If your child hears a story about a brave knight overcoming challenges, they remember the plot and internalize resilience and courage lessons.

Emotion Role Play

Within this section, you and your child will explore activities illuminating how emotions manifest, from the subtle shifts of facial expressions to the intricate dynamics of family interactions and the challenging maze of social engagements. Engaging in these playful exercises will help your child embark on a transformative journey, fostering a greater emotional awareness and a deeper connection to self and others.

Facial Expression Mirror

Faces are the windows to our emotions. A slight raise of an eyebrow, a downturn of the lips, or a twinkle in the eyes can convey feelings more powerfully than words. For children, understanding their facial expressions can be the first step in acknowledging and managing their emotions. *The "Facial Expression Mirror"* activity allows children to explore a spectrum of feelings through their reflections, fostering a deep emotional self-awareness.

Objective:
- To help children identify and understand different emotions through facial expressions.
- To promote self-awareness and the ability to recognize feelings as they arise.
- To build a vocabulary of emotions, bridging the gap between feelings and their outward manifestations.

Best Suited For:
This activity is ideal for children struggling with naming or expressing their emotions. The activity is flexible, making it apt for ages 3 to 9.

Materials Needed:
A large mirror, preferably one that allows both the child and the parent or guardian to view their faces simultaneously.

Instructions:
1. Begin by sitting comfortably with the child in front of the mirror. Take a moment to observe your reflections, noting the neutral expressions.
2. Introduce the idea that our faces can show how we feel on the inside. Mention a few emotions like happiness, sadness, or surprise, and discuss times when the child might have felt them.
3. Start with a basic emotion, like *"happy."* Describe what happens to our faces when we feel this way our eyes brighten, our mouths turn up into a smile, and our cheeks lift. Then, practice making a *"happy"* face in the mirror together.

4. Move on to other emotions, discussing and practicing each one. Delve into more nuanced feelings as you progress. For example, after covering *"sad,"* you might introduce *"disappointed"* or *"lonely."* Describe the subtle differences in expressions for these emotions and practice them together.
5. As you navigate various feelings, ask open-ended questions to make the activity more engaging. For example:
   a. *"How does your face feel when you make an angry expression?"*
   b. *"Can you show me a surprised face and then quickly change it to amused?"*
   c. *"What emotion do you think you most show on your face?"*
6. End the session by asking your child to think of an emotion on their own, portray it with their facial expression, and have them guess it. This reverse activity allows them to be creative and tests their observational skills, making it a fun challenge for both.

Processing the Activity:
- Reflect on the range of emotions covered during the session. Ask the child which expressions they found easy and which were more challenging. This can give insights into the emotions they are more familiar with or those they might be suppressing.
- Encourage them to be mindful of their expressions in real-life scenarios. For instance, if they feel upset, ask them to observe their face in a mirror and see if their outward expression matches their internal feelings.
- Reiterate the importance of facial expressions in communication. Discuss how understanding someone's facial expression can help understand their feelings, fostering empathy and better interpersonal relationships.

Family Dynamics Role-Playing

Family forms the cornerstone of a child's initial understanding of the world. Each member plays a unique role; children often observe, imitate, and absorb the dynamics around them. Through this, children can step into family members' shoes, offering a fresh perspective on relationships, roles, and the emotions tied to them.

Objective:
- To understand and empathize with the roles and feelings of different family members.
- To externalize observations about family dynamics, bringing clarity to interpersonal relationships.
- To enhance communication and connection within the family unit.

Best Suited For:
This activity is tailored for children who might exhibit confusion or distress about certain family situations or those curious about the roles everyone plays at home. Suitable for children who enjoy imaginative role-playing, making it ideal for ages 3 to 9.

Materials Needed:
- Props like hats, scarves, glasses, or accessories represent different family members.
- Printed or drawn pictures of common household scenarios *(e.g., dinner time, watching TV, a family outing)*.
- A safe, open space to act out scenarios.
- Comfortable seating for family members who will be observing.

Instructions:
1. Begin by discussing the various roles within the family, from the nurturing figure of a mother to the playful sibling or the protective father. Let your child know that

everyone has feelings, roles, and responsibilities; it is a dance of balance and understanding.
2. Introduce the props to your child, explaining that each represents a family member. For example, a specific hat could represent grandpa, while a scarf might signify a sister.
3. Present the pictures of household scenarios one by one. Ask your child to choose which family member's role they'd like to play for that particular scenario. As they act out, other family members can join the play, take on their respective roles, or observe.
    - For instance, in a *'dinner time'* scenario, if the child chooses to be the mother, they might start preparing pretend food or calling everyone to the table. Encourage them to mimic voice tones, actions, and emotions they have observed.
4. Allow the role-playing to flow organically, but be prepared to guide or provide prompts if the child seems unsure. For example, you could suggest, *"What would grandpa say about his favorite dish?"* or *"How does big brother react when asked to share?"*
5. Switch roles after a few scenarios, ensuring the child gets an opportunity to step into the shoes of different family members and understand varied perspectives.
6. After the role-playing sessions, gather as a family and discuss the experience. Ask questions like:
    - *"How did it feel to be daddy during bedtime?"*
    - *"What did you notice about being a little sister during playtime?"*
7. Such reflections will help your child articulate observations, feelings, and any revelations they had during the activity.

Processing the Activity:
- Reflect on the roles your child often chose or seemed most intrigued by. This could illuminate certain dynamics they are most curious about or affected by.
- Discuss the real-life parallels of the scenarios acted out. For instance, if a role-played scenario highlighted sharing conflicts between siblings, discuss ways to make sharing more harmonious in real life.
- Revisit the roles and feelings occasionally, asking your child how they perceive changes in family dynamics as days pass. For instance, *"Do you still think mommy gets worried when it's raining?"* or *"How do you feel about grandpa's stories nowadays?*

Social Interaction Improvisation

In the grand theater of life, your children often find themselves navigating various roles, especially regarding their interactions with peers, teachers, or even family. The nuances of social interactions can sometimes be challenging for them to grasp. Through *"Social Interaction Improvisation,"* children can safely explore and practice these dynamics in an imaginative setting, helping them understand and better manage real-life interactions.

Objective:
- To facilitate an understanding of diverse social situations and relationships.
- To provide a platform for practicing appropriate responses and behaviors in various scenarios.
- To foster communication skills, empathy, and confidence in social settings.

Best Suited For:
This improvisational activity is designed for children who might feel uneasy or uncertain in social situations or those looking to boost their social confidence. Fitting for ages 3 to 9.

Materials Needed:
- A collection of cards with different social scenarios written or drawn on them *(e.g., "Meeting a new friend," "Sharing toys," "Saying sorry")*.
- Props or simple costumes *(hats, scarves, badges)* to help set the scene or represent different characters.
- A comfortable, open space for the improvisation to take place.

Instructions:
1. **Start with a warm-up game.** Ask your child to mimic different emotions using facial expressions or body language. This helps them tap into their emotions and sets the stage for the activity.
2. **Introduce the cards, explaining that each one has a unique social situation.** Let the child pick a card at random. Read out the scenario *(or let them interpret the drawing)* and discuss the emotions or actions that might be involved.
3. **Once the scene is set, role-play the situation.** You can be a participant or observer based on the child's comfort. Use the props or costumes to add an element of fun and make the setting more tangible. For instance, if the scenario is *"Being a helper in class,"* a badge might represent the *'helper'* role.
4. **Let the improvisation flow naturally.** If the child seems stuck or uncertain, gently offer prompts or suggestions, guiding them through possible responses or actions. For example, in a *"Sharing toys"* scenario, you could ask, *"How would you ask your friend if you wanted to play with their toy?"*

5. **After acting out a few scenarios, take a moment to reflect.** Discuss the emotions felt, the challenges faced, and the solutions discovered. This reflective conversation is as crucial as the role-playing itself.

Repeat the activity with various scenarios, each time delving deeper into the nuances of social interactions. Over time, introduce more complex situations, helping the child expand their understanding and skills.

Processing the Activity:
- Reflect on the scenarios where the child felt most comfortable and those that posed challenges. This can provide insights into their real-life comfort zones and areas of concern.
- Relate the improvisation to real-life situations. For instance, if a child acted out a scenario about making a new friend, ask them if they have ever felt that way in school or at the park. Drawing parallels between the acted scenarios and real-life experiences reinforces the learning.
- Encourage them to use the lessons from the improvisation in their daily interactions. If they face a challenging situation, remind them of how they tackled it during their role-play.

Therapeutic Puppetry

In play therapy, the magical world of puppetry holds a special place, serving as a bridge between imagination and emotion, play and healing. Puppets, with their animated expressions and vibrant personalities, give children a unique voice, allowing them to explore, understand, and communicate their deepest feelings in a captivating, almost enchanting manner.

Puppet Tales

Storytelling, an age-old tradition, becomes even more compelling when puppets come alive, personifying emotions that young children may grapple with daily. Introducing a child to puppetry and storytelling helps them externalize feelings, offering a safe space to express and reflect.

Objective:
- To allow children to manifest and explore their feelings through characters.
- To cultivate creativity and imaginative narration, enhancing emotional intelligence.
- To encourage the child to understand the complexities of emotions through a story's narrative.

Best Suited For:
Puppet Tales is particularly effective for children who struggle with direct expression or feel more comfortable channeling their feelings through external characters. Perfect for children between 3 and 9, especially those with a penchant for imaginative play.

Materials Needed:
- A selection of hand puppets *(animals, humans, or mystical creatures)*.
- Craft materials: fabric scraps, googly eyes, yarn, glue, and markers to personalize the puppets.
- A simple puppet theater *(can be made using a cardboard box or hanging a blanket)*.
- A small notebook and pen for jotting down the stories.

Instructions:
- Introduce the array of puppets, each representing a specific emotion. For instance, a bluebird might symbolize happiness, while a gray cloud could represent sadness.

- Allow them to feel the texture, play with them, and get acquainted.
- Using the craft materials, invite the child to personalize their puppets. They can add features, decorations, or anything that helps them connect better with the puppet's emotions.
- Once the puppets are ready, it's time to weave a tale. Start with a simple prompt, such as *"Once upon a time, in a vast, green meadow, the bluebird (happiness) and the gray cloud (sadness) met..."* Allow your child to take the reins, manipulating the puppets to bring the story to life.
- As the child navigates the story, encourage them to introduce challenges or situations where the puppets must interact, helping them explore how different emotions react to varying scenarios.
- Each puppet interaction should conclude with a reflection. Ask the child about the story's events, the emotions experienced by the puppets, and if they have ever felt similarly.
- Keep the notebook handy to jot down the stories or significant moments during the play. Over time, these tales can be revisited, serving as a way to gauge the child's evolving emotional understanding.
- After several sessions, the child can invite other family members for a *'puppet show,'* letting them into their world of emotions and fostering a deeper family connection.

Processing the Activity:
- Reflect on the stories narrated. *Which emotion puppet was used the most?*
- Ask open-ended questions about the puppet's adventures. This aids in understanding their perception of emotions and inter-emotional relationships.
- When children manifest real feelings, they relate to their puppet tales. For instance, if they are feeling down, remind

them of how the gray cloud found joy through the help of friends.

Puppetry Emotion Scenarios

The rich imaginary worlds evoked through puppetry engage kids holistically. They can immerse themselves as the puppeteer directing the story while relating to the puppets' emotions. Blending creativity, empathy, and play gives rise to teachable moments not easily replicated through other means.

Objective:
- To provide children a platform to explore and express their feelings through puppet characters.
- To encourage recognition, understanding, and response to different emotional scenarios.
- To develop empathy by considering and enacting varied emotional responses.

Best Suited For:
This activity is designed for children who might be introverted or find direct communication about their feelings challenging. By bringing feelings to the forefront through puppetry, children aged 3 to 9 can navigate their emotional landscapes in a fun, engaging, and non-threatening way.

Materials Needed:
- Various hand puppets *(store-bought or homemade using socks, fabric, and craft supplies)*.
- A simple puppet stage setup *(can be made using a cardboard box or a draped table)*.
- Pre-written cards with different emotional scenarios *(like "A puppet who lost its toy" or "A puppet who's excited about a birthday")*.

Instructions:
1. Set up the puppet stage in a comfortable space, ensuring the child feels relaxed and curious about the upcoming activity. Introduce the puppets to the child, letting them familiarize themselves with each character.
2. Share the objective: together, you will draw scenario cards, and with the chosen puppet, enact how the puppet might feel and react in that situation. Remind them there are no right or wrong portrayals; it is all about exploration.
3. Draw the first card and read the scenario aloud. For instance, *"The puppet feels lonely at a park because no one is playing with it."* Ask the child to select a puppet representing this scenario and act out the emotion. They can give the puppet a voice, express feelings, and maybe even find a resolution.
4. As different scenarios are drawn, encourage the child to switch puppets, delve into varied emotions, and sometimes even challenge them to come up with unexpected reactions. For instance, *what if a puppet, instead of being sad about spilled ice cream, gets excited about the opportunity to choose a new flavor?*
5. Throughout the activity, ensure a balanced mix of positive, negative, and neutral scenarios, giving the child a broad spectrum of emotional situations to engage with.

Processing the Activity:
- Once several scenarios have been enacted, engage in a conversation about the emotions the puppets experienced. *Which scenarios were easy for the child to enact? Which ones posed challenges?*
- Reflect on the varied reactions of the puppets. Discuss that the same situation can elicit different emotions in different individuals.

- Encourage the child to share if they have experienced similar feelings as the puppet in any scenarios in their real life.
- Consider revisiting certain scenarios on subsequent days, seeing if the child enacts them differently, indicating an evolving emotional understanding.

Narrative Healing

Stories have the innate power to heal, validate, and empower. This section delves deep into stories, where emotions are felt, lived, expressed, and understood. Children will embark on a transformative journey, weaving their raw emotions into captivating tales that resonate with their innermost feelings. As these young narrators take the quill, they do more than recount tales; they decode the enigma of their hearts, finding solace, understanding, and a sense of belonging in the magical world of words.

Personal Story Sharing

Every individual, regardless of age, has a unique story to tell. These stories, comprised of experiences, emotions, and personal reflections, shape our worldview and understanding of ourselves. By encouraging children to share their personal stories, we offer them a stage to voice their feelings, dreams, fears, and joys. This *"Personal Story Sharing"* activity invites children to recount moments from their lives, allowing them to practice verbal expression and enhance their emotional vocabulary.

Objective:
- To provide an opportunity for children to express themselves and share personal experiences.
- To foster listening and comprehension skills in children.
- To help children articulate their emotions, strengthening their emotional intelligence.

Best Suited For:
This activity is particularly beneficial for children who might be reserved or reticent. It offers a comfortable space to share their experiences, making them feel valued and heard. Suitable for ages 3 to 9, with stories tailored to their age and comprehension levels.

Materials Needed:
- A comfortable seating arrangement *(cushions, chairs, or mats)*.
- A *"story jar"* filled with prompts or questions to guide the storytelling *(optional)*.
- Visual aids like drawings, photographs, or items could help narrate the story.

Instructions:
1. Begin by creating a calm and inviting environment, ensuring the child feels at ease. Share the purpose of this session: it is their special time to tell any story from their life. It could be about a memorable day, a challenge they faced, a dream, or even an everyday event.
2. If the child is unsure where to start, consider using the *"story jar."* Let them pick a prompt, which could be as simple as *"Tell me about a time you felt happy"* or *"Describe a day when something unexpected happened."* These prompts serve to guide the storytelling, offering a starting point.
3. Encourage them to include as much detail as they wish. Ask open-ended questions to further the narrative, like *"How did that make you feel?"* or *"What happened next?"* Be patient and avoid interrupting. The aim is to let them express themselves freely.
4. If they choose, children can use visual aids to complement their story. A drawing of a family picnic, for instance, can be a great way to talk about family dynamics or a particular outing that meant a lot to them.

5. As the child shares, ensure you are actively listening. Nodding, smiling, or offering encouragement can make a big difference in how they perceive this sharing experience.

Processing the Activity:
- After the storytelling, engage in a brief discussion. Highlight the emotions they mentioned and delve a bit deeper. For instance, if they spoke about a day they felt sad, explore what made them feel better.
- Validate their feelings, ensuring they understand that every emotion is important and natural.
- Encourage them to reflect on the story they shared. *Was it easy or difficult to talk about? How do they feel after sharing it?*
- Assure them that their story is valued and appreciated. This will bolster their confidence and make them more open to sharing in the future.

Emotion Fairy Tales

Every fairy tale spins a story of adventure, emotion, and morals. Similarly, emotions guide our tales, steering us through peaks of joy and valleys of sadness. *"Emotion Fairy Tales"* is an activity that lets children craft their unique fairy tales rooted in feelings. By framing emotions within captivating tales, children are presented with an engaging approach to understanding and articulating their feelings.

Objective:
- To enable children to recognize and communicate various emotions through storytelling.
- To encourage creativity and imagination by crafting unique fairy tales.
- To understand the impact emotions have on actions and decisions within a narrative.

Best Suited For:
Ideal for children who have a vivid imagination and love for tales. This activity bridges their feelings and love for stories, making it suitable for ages 4 to 9.

Materials Needed:
- Blank sheets of paper or a notebook.
- Coloring materials like crayons, colored pencils, or markers.
- Stickers or stamps depicting various emotions *(optional)*.
- Fairy tale props like a magic wand, tiara, or cape for role-playing elements.

Instructions:
1. Start by sharing some popular fairy tales. Highlight moments in these tales where characters felt strong emotions like Cinderella feeling sad or Jack's excitement in *"Jack and the Beanstalk."*
2. Introduce the concept: they will create unique fairy tales, but the story's driving force would be emotions. For instance, *"Once in a land where everyone's shoes depicted their mood, a young prince wore shoes that constantly changed colors. Why was that?"*
3. Ask your kid to select an emotion they would like to explore. Hand them the stickers or stamps, allowing them to choose an emotion visually.
4. Encourage them to draw or write their fairy tale on paper. The fairy tale should have a clear beginning, middle, and end. And the chosen emotion should play a central role in the narrative. For instance, if they chose 'happiness,' maybe their tale could be about a kingdom where laughter was the source of sunlight.
5. Allow them to use the props to act out parts of their story if they wish. Role-playing can help them dive deeper into their character's emotions.

6. Once they've woven their tale, it's sharing time. As they narrate, listen attentively, and engage by asking open-ended questions related to the emotion in focus.

Processing the Activity:
- Explore the challenges the characters faced due to their emotions. Discuss solutions and alternate endings that could have resulted from different emotional reactions.
- Praise their creativity and commend the uniqueness of their fairy tale, boosting their confidence and reinforcing the significance of their feelings.
- Use their fairy tale as a reference in real-life scenarios. For instance, if they feel sad one day, you could say, *"Remember the character in your fairy tale who felt the same? What did they do?"*

Chapter 7
Digital Detox Activities

This offers a variety of creative and engaging activities to help children step away from screens and connect more deeply with the real world. From nature-inspired adventures like scavenger hunts and birdwatching to imaginative crafts and reflective exercises, these activities aim to reignite children's innate curiosity and enhance their sensory experiences. Whether building a cozy indoor fort, documenting favorite memories in a mosaic, or helping devices 'get some sleep,' the chapter provides tools to instill healthy digital habits. The objective is to rediscover the joys of unplugged play and forge meaningful human connections.

Identifying Screen Dependency

In the hyper-connected digital era, screens are a significant part of our daily lives. From smartphones to laptops, tablets to gaming consoles, screens are everywhere. As screens become more ingrained in our routines, understand the potential implications of excessive screen time on their children and to be able to identify signs of screen dependency.

Screen Time Monitoring

Understanding screen time is the first step to monitoring its use. As a parent, consider this: *How often does your child reach for their device? Do they seem restless without it?*

Imagine Sarah, a 9-year-old who enjoyed playing with her dolls and drawing. Lately, however, her parents have noticed she's always on her tablet, watching videos or playing games. They rarely see her engaged in her old favorite activities. They decided to take note of her screen time for a week and realized she was spending over 5 hours daily on her device.

Parents like Sarah's can get a clearer picture of their child's relationship with screens by monitoring screen time.

Tips for Monitoring:
- **Maintain a log:** Write down the start and end times whenever your child uses a screen.
- **Use built-in tools:** Many devices have screen time tracking features that give detailed breakdowns of app usage.
- **Set boundaries:** If screen time is excessive, discuss it with your child and establish designated screen-free periods.

The Impact on Social Skills

While screens offer educational and entertainment value, excessive screen time can impact a child's social skills. Face-to-face interactions are fundamental for developing empathy, understanding non-verbal cues, and cultivating genuine human relationships. Here are some consequences of excessive screen time on social skills:

- **Reduced Empathy:** Children might struggle to understand others' feelings.
- **Limited Understanding of Non-verbal Cues:** Overreliance on text and emojis can reduce the ability to interpret facial expressions and body language.
- **Struggle with Real-life Conversations:** Conversations on screens can be edited and filtered, but real conversations cannot.

Recognizing Warning Signs

Screen dependency does not just pop up overnight. There are warning signs that, if identified early, can help address the issue.

- **Mood Swings:** If your child becomes irritable or upset when their screen time is reduced or interrupted, this could be a sign.
- **Loss of Interest in Other Activities:** Just like Sarah, it is worth noting if a child suddenly loses interest in activities they once loved.
- **Neglecting Responsibilities:** Homework left undone or chores ignored because they're engrossed in screen activities is a warning sign.
- **Secretive Behavior:** If your child hides their screen when you approach or lies about the time spent, it is a sign of dependency.

Activities Away from Screens

These activities are not your ordinary games. They are bridges to the world beyond pixels and sounds. They invite young minds to touch, feel, observe, and interact with the world in its rawest form. Whether it's the rustling of leaves underfoot, the cool architecture of a home-built sanctuary, or the gentle flutter of a bird's wing, these engagements nurture a child's connection to the world, sharpening their senses and broadening their horizons. Dive in, and let your child discover the magic beyond the screen.

Nature Scavenger Hunt

Embarking on a journey through nature allows children to connect deeply with the world around them. Through the Nature Scavenger Hunt, children will harness their observation and exploration skills while fostering a sense of wonder and respect for their environment.

Objective:
- To heighten sensory awareness and observational skills.
- To foster a sense of curiosity and connection to the natural world.
- To promote physical activity and exploration in a playful manner.

Best Suited For:
Children between the ages of 3 to 9, especially those who seem disengaged from their surroundings or have a strong inclination towards screens. This activity is particularly beneficial in spring or fall, when nature undergoes significant changes, offering many items to discover.

Materials Needed:
- A handcrafted list or printed checklist of items to find.
- A basket or bag for collecting items.
- A camera or smartphone *(optional)* for capturing findings.
- Small magnifying glass to examine treasures up close.

The Nature Scavenger Hunt Activity:
1. Draft a list of items that children should look for during the hunt. This can include specific leaves, flowers, insects, or any natural item like a pinecone, feather, or smooth rock. The list can be illustrated with pictures for younger children, while older kids can have written clues or riddles leading to the item.
2. Before heading out, sit with the child and discuss the list, asking them what each item might look or feel like. This builds anticipation and excitement.
3. Head outdoors, in a backyard, park, or forest. Allow the child to lead the way, exploring and observing. Remind them that the aim is not just to collect, notice, and appreciate nature's intricacies.

- For items too big or inappropriate to collect, like a bird or a squirrel, kids can point them out or snap a photo if you have a camera.
4. As your kid discovers each item, engage in discussions.
    - *How does the pinecone feel? Is it rough or smooth?*
    - *Why do you think birds have feathers? Can you feel the softness?*
    - *What colors can you see on the smooth rock? How do you think it got so smooth?*
5. Once the hunt is over, lay out all the found items. Discuss each one, appreciating its uniqueness and role in nature. For collected photographs, you can view them together, reminiscing about the adventure.

Processing the Activity:
- Reflect on the adventure, asking the child about their favorite discovery and why it stood out to them.
- Discuss the importance of preserving nature, emphasizing the idea of *'look, do not touch'* for certain items or creatures, ensuring they understand the balance of exploration and respect.
- Revisit the hunt after a few months, noticing seasonal changes and appreciating nature's ever-evolving beauty.

Build a Fort

Every child dreams of having a secret space to call their own, a little hideaway where they can dream, play, and let their imagination run wild. Building a fort offers them this special space and nurtures their problem-solving abilities, spatial reasoning, and imaginative prowess. By creating a sanctuary using everyday household items, children delve deep into a world of creativity, where the living room transforms into a castle, jungle hideout, or spaceship.

Objective:
- To harness and enhance children's imaginative and creative faculties.
- To foster problem-solving and decision-making abilities.
- To develop spatial understanding as children determine how to construct and stabilize their fort.

Best Suited For:
Ideal for children aged 3 to 9 who enjoy role-playing and storytelling or those who seem confined by structured play. Particularly effective on rainy or colder days when outdoor activities are limited, turning indoor confinement into an adventure.

Materials Needed:
- Blankets, sheets, or large towels.
- Pillows and cushions.
- Chairs, sofas, or sturdy tables.
- String lights *(optional)* for added ambiance.
- Clips or clothespins to secure blankets in place.

Instructions:
1. Settle on the kind of fort they would like to construct. *Is it a royal castle, a secret superhero base, or perhaps a deep-sea underwater cave?* Knowing the theme can guide the building process.
2. Identify the primary furniture pieces to act as the fort's foundation. Tables provide an overhead structure, while sofas and chairs offer cornerstones.
3. Drape blankets or sheets over the chosen furniture. Use clips or clothespins to ensure the blankets remain in place. If building a multi-room fort, use separate blankets for each section.
4. Inside the fort, line the floor with pillows and cushions, making it a cozy haven for the child. Add a few stuffed animals or toys relevant to the fort's theme.

5. If you have string lights, they can be intertwined with the blankets to create a starry effect, especially if the fort's theme is a nighttime adventure or space odyssey.
6. Once the fort is built, engage in themed activities within it. *If it is a castle, could you have a royal tea party?* For a space-themed fort, discuss the planets or imagine an alien encounter.
7. Over several days, encourage your child to modify and adapt the fort. This iterative process reinforces problem-solving as they rethink and redesign their structure.
8. Once inside the fort, it is a perfect setting for stories. Share tales that align with the fort's theme or let the child craft their narratives based on their creation.

Processing the Activity:
- Ask about the stories or games they played inside the fort. This provides insight into their imaginative world, understanding their fears, aspirations, and dreams.
- Offer praise for their creativity and resourcefulness. Highlight specific instances where they showcased problem-solving or unique thinking.
- Consider documenting the fort-building process with photos. Over time, these can be compiled, showcasing the evolution of their architectural creativity.

Bird Watching

Pausing to admire nature can be profoundly therapeutic for children. Bird watching is not only an opportunity to connect with the environment but also an exercise in patience, observation, and presence. As children scan the skies or treetops, they learn to wait, observe, and appreciate the subtle wonders of the natural world.

Objective:
- To enhance observation skills and boost attention to detail.
- To nurture patience as they wait to spot different birds.
- To foster a deeper appreciation and connection to the natural world.

Best Suited For:
Ideal for children aged 4 to 9, especially those who might be restless or easily distracted. Bird-watching activity is a great way to introduce moments of mindfulness and can be especially calming for children with high energy or anxiety levels.

Materials Needed:
- A pair of child-friendly binoculars.
- A basic bird identification chart or book, preferably with illustrations.
- A notepad or journal for recording observations.
- Colored pencils or crayons for drawing.

Instructions:
1. Ensure your child understands the activity by briefly explaining what bird watching entails. Let them know it is about patience, quietness, and keen observation.
2. Teach them how to use the binoculars—focusing on distant objects and adjusting the lens to get a clear view.
3. Introduce them to the bird identification chart or book. Highlight a few common birds they might encounter in your area.
4. Find a comfortable spot in your yard, balcony, or park. It should be quiet and preferably where birds are often seen.
5. Encourage them to be still and silent, using their eyes and ears. They should listen to bird calls and try to spot the bird using their binoculars.

6. Once they spot a bird, they can refer to the identification chart to recognize it. In their notepad, they can jot down the name of the bird, its color, size, and any distinct features. If inclined, they can even draw a picture of it.
7. After a set period, discuss what they observed. *Which birds did they find most intriguing? Were there any they could not identify?*
8. Over time, extend the bird-watching sessions. You can even plan visits to bird sanctuaries or other environments to observe different species.

Processing the Activity:
- Discuss the behaviors they observed. *For instance, was a particular bird hopping around? Was another pecking at a tree?* This encourages keen observation and understanding of nature.
- If they drew pictures, show appreciation for their artwork. Discuss the colors, shapes, and patterns they observed. This not only validates their efforts but also boosts their confidence.
- If possible, make bird watching a regular activity. Over time, this can become a calming routine, teaching patience and observation in other aspects of life.

Establishing Healthy Screen Habits

Internet and other digital devices have become integral to children's daily lives. Yet, just as a painter must learn when to step back from the canvas, so must your young ones learn the art of digital moderation.

Device Sleeping Bags

In today's digital age, screen time is an inherent part of children's lives, and it is crucial to teach the concept of boundaries and self-discipline regarding electronic devices. Just as our bodies need sleep to rejuvenate, devices, too, metaphorically speaking, benefit from rest. This activity serves dual purposes: it offers a tactile, hands-on crafting experience while emphasizing the importance of balancing screen time and rest. Engaging children in such activities sparks their creativity and teaches them essential life skills in a fun and interactive way.

Objective:
- To instill the concept of healthy boundaries with electronic devices.
- To develop patience, discipline, and creative skills through crafting.
- To help children understand the importance of rest both for themselves and the tools they use.

Best Suited For:
Children ages 5 to 9 often use tablets, phones, or other electronic devices, especially before bedtime. It is an activity designed not just to encourage creative expression but also to instill responsible digital habits.

Materials Needed:
- Fabric or felt in various colors
- Ribbons, buttons, or sequins for decoration
- Scissors *(safety scissors for younger children)*
- Fabric glue or a simple sewing kit
- Markers for customization
- A measuring tape or ruler

Instructions:
1. Begin by discussing with your child how everything, even non-living things, benefits from rest. Draw parallels between how they feel after a good night's sleep and how their device might *"feel."*

2. Measure the device that your child frequently uses. Add an extra inch to these measurements to ensure the device fits comfortably inside its new sleeping bag.
3. Cut out two rectangles from the fabric using the measurements you have taken. Doing so will form the front and back of the sleeping bag.
4. Allow the child to decorate one side of one of the rectangles—this will be the front. They can use markers, buttons, ribbons, or any other craft supplies you have on hand. Maybe they would like to draw a dream cloud, stars, or a calming night scene on it.
5. Once the decorations are dry or firmly attached, place the two rectangles together, with the decorated side facing outward.
    - For the non-sewing version, use fabric glue to bond the edges of three sides, leaving the top open. A simple stitch along three sides will suffice for those who want to sew.
6. Once your bag is ready, discuss the importance of *"tucking the device in"* at a particular time each night. Establishing this ritual can be fun; perhaps the device gets a bedtime story some nights or a lullaby.
7. As days progress, you can add elements like making a tiny pillow or blanket for the device, enhancing the bedtime routine, and further driving home the metaphor.

Processing the Activity:
1. At the end of a week or two, sit with your child and discuss how the bedtime routine for their device is going. *Do they find it easier to sleep? Do they feel better knowing their device is "resting," too?*
2. Talk about how routines and habits can help us in life. Just as their device has a bedtime, emphasize the importance of their bedtime routine.

3. Discuss the feelings and thoughts that arise when they are not constantly plugged in before sleep. Perhaps they have begun noticing they dream more or feel more rested.

Screen Time Storyboard

With the increasing role screens play in children's lives, they need to understand the content they are consuming and its impact on their emotions and understanding of the world. The screen time storyboard activity provides a tangible and creative platform for children to express and reflect on their screen time experiences. By visualizing their daily digital interactions, children can boost their creative skills and cultivate mindfulness regarding the nature and quality of their screen time.

Objective:
- To foster a sense of reflection on the content children engage with during screen time.
- To enhance their storytelling and artistic abilities.
- To promote conscious decisions regarding future screen content choices based on their storyboard reflections.

Best Suited For:
Children between the ages of 4 and 9 who have routine screen interactions through educational apps, cartoons, games, or any other digital media. It assists children in making sense of the content they're exposed to and encourages them to be selective and intentional about their screen choices.

Materials Needed:
- Blank storyboard templates *(a simple grid on paper will suffice, one box for each day of the week)*.
- Crayons, colored pencils, markers, or watercolors.
- Stickers or stamps *(optional)*.
- A journal or folder to keep their weekly storyboards.

Instructions:
1. Initiate a conversation with your child about their favorite screen time activities. Discuss the various shows, apps, or games they engage with and ask them about the stories or lessons they have taken away from them.
2. Present them with a blank storyboard template. Explain that every day, after their designated screen time, they will have a chance to draw or write about what they watched, played, or learned.
3. Encourage them to be as detailed or as imaginative as they like. They can recreate scenes and characters or even develop alternative endings or scenarios.
4. At the end of each day, spend a few minutes discussing their storyboard entry. Ask them questions to promote deeper reflection:
    - *Why did they choose to depict that particular scene or character?*
    - *How did what they watched or played make them feel?*
    - *Was there something new they learned or found interesting?*
5. As the week progresses, you may notice your child becoming more discerning about their screen choices, opting for the content they are excited to add to their storyboard.
6. At the end of the week, review the storyboard together. Look for themes or patterns. *Did they focus a lot on one particular show or game? Were there varied emotions across the week?*

Processing the Activity:
- Reflect on the week's storyboard. *What insights can be drawn about your child's screen preferences?*
- Discuss the importance of balance in screen content – the mix of entertainment, education, creativity, and relaxation.
- Encourage your child to set intentions for the next week. Based on their storyboard, *is there something new they would like to explore? Or is it something they would want to revisit?*

- Use the storyboard as a guide to introduce them to new content that aligns with their interests and offers new learning or perspectives.

Memory Mosaic

Children can easily become absorbed in the virtual world, sometimes missing out on the beautiful real-world experiences around them. The Memory Mosaic activity is a craft-based play therapy that encourages kids to recognize and cherish their offline experiences, emphasizing the importance of connections and memories made without screens. Through this craft, children will not only celebrate their most cherished real-life moments but will also be inspired to seek more of such experiences in the future.

Objective:
- To acknowledge and appreciate moments and connections made outside the digital world.
- To stimulate creativity and hands-on crafting skills.
- To emphasize the importance of balance between online and offline experiences.

Best Suited For:
Children between the ages of 4 and 9 who lean heavily on digital platforms for entertainment or social connections. Designed to remind them of the joy and importance of real-life experiences and connections. Ideal for those who enjoy arts and crafts.

Materials Needed:
- A large piece of poster board or canvas.
- Magazines, family photos, or printed pictures of memorable moments.
- Glue, scissors, and coloring supplies like crayons, colored pencils, or markers.
- Decorative items like glitter, buttons, ribbons, and stickers.

Instructions:
1. Sit with your child and start a conversation about their favorite offline memories. These could be family vacations, picnics, visits to the zoo, birthday parties, or simple everyday moments like reading a book together or playing in the park.
2. Ask them to choose a handful of these memories they want to feature on their Memory Mosaic. Use printed photographs of these moments or ask them to illustrate them if possible.
3. Hand them the large poster board or canvas and explain that this will be their canvas to create a beautiful mosaic of their offline memories.
4. Allow them to cut out pictures from magazines, family photos, or drawings that resonate with their chosen memories.
5. Encourage them to glue these images onto the board in any arrangement they like. They can overlap, place them side by side, or even create a collage.
6. Once they have positioned all their images, let them decorate the spaces in between with coloring supplies, glitter, buttons, and any other decorative items. This will add a personal touch to their mosaic.
7. Once the mosaic is complete, discuss each image or drawing. Dive deep into the emotions felt during those moments, the people involved, and why they cherish that memory.

Processing the Activity:
- Hang the Memory Mosaic in a prominent place in your home to serve as a constant reminder of the beautiful offline moments in life.
- Initiate discussions about the balance between screen time and real-life experiences, highlighting the importance of both.

- Encourage your child to regularly update or create new Memory Mosaics as they make more offline memories.
- Plan future offline activities inspired by the memories they have chosen to feature. This can be a great way to ensure they continue seeking and cherishing real-world experiences.

Chapter 8
Self-Control and Concentration Activities

This chapter provides insights and activities aimed at boosting the valuable skills of self-control and concentration in kids. It begins by highlighting the multitude of benefits that can come from enhancing self-control, concentration, and patience in children. It emphasizes how these skills pave the way for better relationships, academic excellence, and an overall capability to handle life's ups and downs. The chapter then discusses various play therapy techniques and games focused on building mindfulness, emotional regulation, and mental focus. Breathing exercises, guided meditation, sensory play, and therapeutic crafts equip children with tools to manage their emotions, focus their attention, and nurture their inner resilience.

Benefits of Boosting Self-Control

Patience, concentration, and self-control are not emphasized in the fast-paced world. These are skills that, when honed, can revolutionize the way a person interacts with the world, leading to a host of benefits. For children, especially, these skills can pave the way for better relationships, academic success, and a robust ability to handle life's curveballs. Through play therapy activities, you can give your children the tools they need to build these invaluable skills.

Develops Focus and Patience

Imagine your child in a situation where they are tempted to grab a toy from a friend. Instead of acting impulsively, they take a deep breath, wait, and ask if they can play with it. That is the magic of self-control. Children can navigate their impulses and choose a more constructive action with improved focus.

Enhances Academic Performance

The benefits of self-control are not confined to personal interactions. In the academic realm, children with better self-control tend to excel. *Why?* Because learning often requires patience, focus, and the ability to resist distractions.

Building Resilience and Adaptability

Life is unpredictable. It is filled with ups and downs, joys and challenges. For a child, navigating these changes can be daunting. However, a strong sense of self-control can be their compass. It allows them to adapt to new situations, bounce back from disappointments, and handle stress more effectively.

Mindfulness Activities

During childhood, when dreams intertwine with reality, and emotions often wear vivid hues, offering children a compass to navigate their inner selves. Mindfulness activities act as this guiding compass, illuminating pathways to self-awareness, presence, and tranquility.

Breathing and Grounding Techniques

Engaging in craft activities can offer not only a fun diversion but also a meaningful way to embed these techniques into their daily life. This craft activity revolves around creating a *"Breath Bracelet,"* a tangible reminder for children to practice deep breathing and grounding when they feel overwhelmed or anxious.

Objective:
- To equip children with a creative tool that prompts them to practice deep breathing and grounding.
- To instill the importance of mindfulness and being present in the moment.
- To cultivate a sense of ownership over their emotions and responses.

Best Suited For:
Children aged 3 to 9, especially those who may experience anxiety, restlessness, or emotional outbursts. The activity provides a tactile reminder to breathe and ground themselves, making it beneficial when they need self-soothing.

Materials Needed:
- Assorted beads *(preferably larger ones for younger children)*
- Elastic string
- A special centerpiece bead *(this could be a unique shape or color)*
- Scissors
- A piece of paper and markers

Instructions:
1. Begin by discussing with your child the importance of deep breathing. Explain how it can help calm their mind and body. Mention that the bracelet will serve as a reminder to practice this technique.

2. Invite your child to pick a centerpiece bead. This bead represents a full, deep breath. Every time they see or touch it, it will be a reminder to take a moment to breathe deeply.
3. Lay out the assorted beads and ask your child to choose several. Each bead they add represents one breath cycle: inhale and exhale. The number of beads can depend on the age of the child; younger children might choose fewer beads, while older children might add more.
4. Thread the centerpiece bead onto the elastic string first, then have your child add the other beads, one by one, while practicing a breath for each.
5. When the bracelet is filled with beads, tie it off securely. The bracelet should be easy to slip on and off the child's wrist.
6. With the piece of paper and markers, invite your child to write or draw what they feel when calm or after they've practiced deep breathing. This becomes a visual representation of their calm state.
7. Encourage your child to wear the bracelet daily or keep it somewhere accessible. Whenever they touch the centerpiece bead or any other bead, they should be reminded to pause and take deep breaths.

Processing the Activity:
- Ask your child how they felt when they took a breath for each bead. *Did they notice a change in how their body or mind felt?*
- Discuss the significance of the centerpiece bead. Emphasize its role as a special reminder for grounding and centering themselves.
- Whenever your child experiences heightened emotions, gently point to their bracelet or ask if they have used it as a reminder to breathe deeply.
- Over time, observe if your child naturally uses the bracelet as a tool for self-regulation. Celebrate these moments and validate their efforts.

Sensory Exploration

The world is a mosaic of sensations, from the rough texture of a tree bark to the gentle caress of a breeze. Engaging our senses is a journey of discovery and understanding. For children, sensory exploration is not just about recognizing the different textures, smells, or sounds; it is about connecting with their environment, understanding their reactions to stimuli, and cultivating self-awareness. Crafting a *"Sensory Storybook"* provides children with an interactive way to explore, document, and reflect on various sensations they encounter daily.

Objective:
- To promote sensory awareness and recognition in children.
- To encourage documentation and reflection on various sensory experiences.
- To foster creativity and self-expression through crafting.

Best Suited For:
Children aged 3 to 9 who are curious about the world around them or those who may benefit from heightened sensory awareness due to sensory processing challenges. This activity can be especially therapeutic for children who might need a structured approach to sensory exploration.

Materials Needed:
- Blank notebook or scrapbook
- Various craft materials such as fabric swatches *(velvet, cotton, sandpaper, etc.)*, scented stickers or scratch-and-sniff elements, bells, or other sound-making items
- Glue, scissors, markers, colored pencils, and crayons
- Stamps, ink pads in various colors
- Everyday items from nature like leaves, petals, or twigs

Instructions:
1. If your child is unfamiliar, Introduce the five senses: sight, sound, smell, touch, and taste. Mention that the book they will craft will include pages dedicated to each of these senses.
2. Start with the *'Touch'* section. Have your child select fabric swatches and everyday items and glue them onto a page. As they touch each item, ask them to describe the texture and their feelings.
3. Move on to the 'Smell' section. Use scented stickers or, if safe, items like herbs *(lavender, mint)* glued to the page. Let the child smell and describe the scent, and document it.
4. For the *'Sight'* section, invite them to draw or color a picture of something they love to see or use stamps and ink pads to create patterns. Discuss the colors and shapes they have chosen.
5. The *'Sound'* section might be a bit trickier, but use creativity. Maybe they can draw representations of their favorite sounds, or you could attach small bells or other items that make a noise.
6. For *'Taste,"* instead of actual food items, have them draw or use stickers of their favorite foods. Alternatively, they can cut out images from magazines. Discuss why they like those particular tastes.
7. Throughout the creation of the storybook, encourage your child not just to experience but to document. For instance, they could write or draw how it makes them feel next to a fabric swatch. By a picture of their favorite food, they might describe the taste as *"sweet like a summer day."*

Processing the Activity:
- Encourage your child to share the storybook with other family members, explaining their choice. This can help in boosting their communication skills and confidence.

- Keep the Sensory Storybook accessible and revisit it periodically. As they grow, their sensory preferences and perceptions might change, and it can be insightful to add more pages or create a new book.
- In moments when the child might feel overwhelmed or anxious, use the book as a grounding tool. Have them turn to their favorite page and focus on that sensation, helping them divert their attention and calm down.

Guided Meditation

In a world bustling with stimuli, offering children a space to retreat mentally can be immensely beneficial. Meditation serves as an excellent tool for fostering self-control and concentration. Guided meditation, specifically tailored for children, can take them on magical journeys while remaining rooted in one spot, enhancing their ability to focus and remain calm. Through this activity, children will embark on a fantastical journey, nurturing their imaginative abilities and honing concentration.

Objective:
- To introduce children to meditation as a means to develop self-control.
- To cultivate concentration and mindfulness.
- To nurture imaginative faculties and provide an escape from daily overstimulation.

Best Suited For:
Children aged 3 to 9 may be struggling with attention, easily distracted, or those who are quite imaginative and love to daydream. It can be a way to channel their energy constructively. Particularly helpful when children need calming or before bedtime to ensure restful sleep.

Materials Needed:
- A quiet, comfortable space free of distractions.
- Soft floor mat or cushion for the child to sit or lie down.
- Gentle background instrumental music *(optional)*.
- A script for the guided meditation *(which will be provided below)*.

Instructions:
1. Prepare the environment by ensuring the room is comfortably lit, not too bright or dim. If using, start the gentle instrumental music, making sure it is at a soothing volume.
2. Have the child sit down comfortably on the mat or cushion. They can either sit cross-legged or lie down, whichever they prefer.
3. Begin with some deep breaths. Ask the child to inhale deeply, hold for a second, and exhale slowly. Do this a few times until you see them starting to relax.
4. Start the guided meditation:

"Close your eyes and imagine standing at the entrance of a beautiful forest. The trees are tall and majestic, their leaves shimmering in colors you have never seen before. As you walk, you feel the soft grass beneath your feet. Can you feel it?

Ahead, you see a gentle stream of crystal clear and sparkling water. You walk over and dip your feet in, feeling the cool water. It is refreshing and calming. Nearby, a friendly deer comes over to greet you. It nudges you playfully and beckons you to follow.

The deer leads you to a hidden part of the forest where magical creatures live. There is a group of playful fairies dancing around, their wings glittering. A kind old wizard sits on a rock, reading a book that floats in the air. He looks at you and, with a smile, conjures a beautiful floating orb of light. The orb gently circles you, and with each rotation, you feel more and more relaxed.

As you continue exploring, you come across a calm, serene meadow. The grass is soft, and the flowers emit a gentle glow. You decide to lie down here, feeling completely safe and at peace. The sky above is filled with stars, each twinkling just for you.

Remember, in this magical land, you are safe, loved, and can return anytime. When you are ready, slowly wiggle your fingers and toes, bringing awareness back to where you are. When you feel ready, open your eyes."

5. Once finished guiding them through this journey, allow your child a few minutes of quiet to process the experience. The peacefulness and imagery can help them anchor themselves in moments of restlessness.

Processing the Activity:
- Once they open their eyes, discuss the journey with them. Ask them what they saw, felt, or heard. *Were there parts of the story they particularly loved?*
- Discuss the feeling of calm and relaxation. Ask them to compare how they felt before and after the meditation. *Do they feel more at ease and more focused?*
- Encourage them to visit their magical land whenever they need to escape and focus. Remind them that this special place is just for them, and they can shape it however they like.

Focus-Based Games

Focus-based games offer children a direct way to understand and manage their emotions. Through playful tools and activities, kids learn to center their attention, process their feelings, and harness their inner calm.

Concentration Card Games

A deck of cards, often seen as a tool for simple games or magic tricks, can be transformed into a concentration-enhancing tool for young minds. Engaging in card games not only helps children build cognitive skills but also helps them develop patience, strategy, and a keen focus.

Objective:
- To enhance children's concentration and memory skills.
- To teach patience and turn-taking, which are essential for self-control.
- To introduce strategic thinking and observation.

Best Suited For:
This card game is ideal for children aged 4 to 9, especially those who are easily distracted or enjoy visual challenges. It is an excellent activity for rainy days, quiet afternoons, or any time your child needs a focused break from screen time.

Materials Needed:
- A deck of standard playing cards or specially designed children's cards with vivid images.
- A quiet space with a table or flat surface to play.

Instructions:
1. Shuffle the cards well. Consider using just the numbers *(remove face cards)* for younger children to keep it simpler when using standard playing cards. For older kids, the entire deck can be used.
2. Lay out the cards face-down in a grid pattern. The grid's size can vary based on the child's age and familiarity with card games. For younger kids, start with a 3x4 grid *(12 cards);* for older ones, you can use a 4x4 or even 5x5 grid.

3. The game's goal is simple: to find matching pairs of cards by turning over two cards at a time. The challenge is to remember the location of each card as they are revealed.
4. The child begins by flipping over any two cards. If they match *(in number or image, depending on the card type)*, the cards are removed from the grid. If they do not match, they are turned back face-down to their original positions.
5. The game continues with the child flipping over two cards at a time, trying to find matching pairs based on memory.
6. As the game progresses, encourage them to take their time, concentrate, and try to recall the position of previously revealed cards. This exercise strengthens memory and focus.
7. For added challenge and to introduce turn-taking, parents or guardians can join in the game, taking turns with the child to find matching pairs. This introduces an element of competition, making the game even more engaging and teaching the child about patience and waiting for their turn.
8. The game ends when all matching pairs have been found and removed from the grid.

Processing the Activity:
- After the game, ask your child the strategies they employed. *Did they have a particular method, or was it random? Did they start from one end of the grid and move systematically?*
- For continuous improvement, you can time how long it takes to complete the game and challenge them to improve their time in subsequent plays, ensuring they remain focused.
- The game can be more challenging by increasing the grid size, introducing more diverse cards, or adding additional rules *(like a time limit for each turn)*.
- Praise your child for their effort and concentration. Celebrate the improvements in their memory and focus.

I Spy

The classic "I Spy" game is more than just a fun pastime—it explores details and challenges a child's observational skills. Diving deep into the details enhances a child's focus and patience and reinforces their capability to be present in the moment and observe the world with a keen eye.

Objective:
- To enhance a child's observational skills, attention to detail, and patience.
- To encourage children to appreciate the little things and stay present in the moment.
- To foster a bond between the parent or guardian and the child through shared experiences.

Best Suited For:
Children aged 4 to 9 who have a natural curiosity and those who can benefit from sharpening their focus and observational skills. This activity is especially helpful for kids who tend to get distracted easily or have difficulty staying attentive.

Materials Needed:
- Various rooms or settings, each with distinct objects.
- Paper and pencils or crayons *(for an added drawing challenge)*.

Expanded I Spy Activity:
1. Begin in a familiar setting, like the living room. State the rules of the traditional *"I Spy"* game for clarity.
2. Start the game by choosing an object without revealing its identity. Say, *"I spy with my little eye something that is [color]."*
3. As the child starts guessing, give them three attempts to identify the object. If they cannot guess it in three tries, reveal the object to them.

4. After the first few rounds, add layers of complexity. For example, *"I spy with my little eye something that is [color] and has a texture of [smooth/rough/etc.]"* or *"I spy something that is [shape] and is used for [function]."*
5. Transition to different settings, such as a bedroom, kitchen, or outdoors. Each change in the environment offers a fresh set of challenges.
6. For an added twist, hand them paper and pencils or crayons after the child identifies several objects. Ask them to draw the objects they have identified, paying attention to the color, shape, and any specific details they remember.
7. Play multiple rounds, and as the child becomes more proficient, reduce the number of hints or clues given or increase the complexity of the clues.
8. End the game by discussing the objects they observed, appreciated, or found challenging to identify. Probe into why they think they missed some objects and how they felt when they couldn't immediately identify certain items.

Processing the Activity:
- Reflect on the entire experience. Ask the child which round or setting was the most challenging and why.
- Discuss the importance of patience.
- Talk about the drawing aspect of the game *(if you included it). How did the child feel about representing their observations on paper? Did drawing help them remember details better?*
- Praise their observational skills and the details they managed to pick up. Reinforce the idea that the world is full of tiny wonders and details waiting to be observed.
- Suggest making *"I Spy"* a regular activity, even without it being a structured game. For instance, when walking, in the car, or during other daily activities. The world is filled with details, and this game can be a way of staying connected to the present moment.

Emotional Regulation Strategies

Childhood emotions can sometimes resemble towering waves, ready to crash at any moment. But within every young heart, there is a reservoir of resilience and understanding waiting to be tapped. Emotional regulation strategies serve as guiding beacons, helping children decipher, manage, and even surf these emotional waves with grace and skill.

Worry Monster

The concept of a Worry Monster is a playful way for kids to externalize their concerns. By crafting their monsters and feeding them with their troubles, kids get an engaging method to face and control their feelings.

Objective:
- To provide a creative outlet for children to express and manage their worries.
- To enable children to visualize their concerns as something external and controllable.
- To offer a tactile experience that can help in understanding and processing feelings.

Best Suited For:
This activity is especially helpful for children who tend to internalize their concerns, leading to anxiety or stress. It can be a game-changer for those between 4 and 9 years old who might struggle to articulate their worries.

Materials Needed:
- Craft paper or fabric in various colors.
- Craft supplies: googly eyes, buttons, glue, scissors, yarn for hair, etc.
- Markers, crayons, or colored pencils.
- Small notes or papers.

Instructions:
1. Explain to your child what worries are. Explain that everyone has worries from time to time, but sometimes, talking about them or finding a way to deal with them can help.
2. Introduce the idea of the Worry Monster. Describe it as a friendly monster that loves to eat up all the worries, making them disappear.
3. Invite your child to design their own Worry Monster. They can draw a picture of it on craft paper or use fabric to make a small stuffed toy-like version. Encourage them to make it as colorful, silly, or imaginative as they want. The more unique, the better!
4. As they craft, casually discuss some common worries kids might have – like a scary dream, a tough day at school, or worries about a new experience. This will give them context without pressuring them to open up.
5. Once the monster is crafted, introduce the small notes or papers. Whenever your child feels worried, they can write or draw their concern on paper.
6. Feed the worries to the Worry Monster. Fold the worry note for paper drawing and place it in the monster's mouth. Create a small pocket or slot representing the monster's mouth for the fabric version.
7. Sit down with your child every few days or once a week to *"check"* on the monster. Take out the worries and discuss them. Some might not seem as big anymore. Others may need more discussion. Decide together if the monster needs to eat them again or if they can be thrown away.
8. Over time, this playful ritual helps make discussing worries a regular activity, ensuring that feelings do not accumulate and become overwhelming.

Processing the Activity:
- Reflect together on how the Worry Monster is helping. *Are there fewer worries now? Do the worries seem smaller after the monster eats them?*
- Discuss the importance of sharing feelings and concerns. While the Worry Monster is a fun way to manage worries, talking to someone they trust, like a parent or guardian, is also beneficial.
- If your child becomes particularly attached to their Worry Monster, consider bringing it to significant events or transitions. It can be a familiar tool to help process new or overwhelming feelings.

Soothing Scented Playdough

Playdough is a tactile delight for children and offers countless opportunities for creativity, motor skill development, and therapeutic healing. Combined with calming scents, it creates a multi-sensory experience that can harness a child's attention and induce relaxation. Through the Soothing Scented Playdough activity, children mold imaginative shapes and take in the calming aromas that help in emotional grounding.

Objective:
- To harness focus and concentration through tactile play.
- To provide sensory relaxation with the help of calming scents.
- To combine creative expression and therapeutic benefits in one activity.

Best Suited For:
Children aged between 3 and 9, especially those who might be hyperactive, anxious, or have difficulty focusing on tasks. The scents and tactile nature of the playdough make it ideal for children who benefit from sensory-based interventions.

Materials Needed:
- Basic playdough ingredients: flour, salt, cream of tartar, water, and cooking oil.
- Calming essential oils: Lavender is popular, but chamomile or light vanilla can work.
- Natural food coloring *(optional for added visual appeal)*.
- Playdough tools: Rolling pins, cutters, and molds.

Instructions:
1. Begin by preparing the playdough. Mix two cups of flour with half a cup of salt and two tablespoons of cream of tartar in a large mixing bowl.
2. Mix 1.5 cups of warm water in a separate bowl with a tablespoon of cooking oil and a few drops of your chosen essential oil.
3. Slowly blend the wet mixture into the dry ingredients. If you are using natural food coloring, add it now. Stir until it forms a dough-like consistency.
4. Knead the dough on a floured surface until smooth. When it is too sticky, add a bit more flour.
5. Once the playdough is ready, invite your child to play with it. Encourage them to take deep breaths as they play, helping them notice the scent. The act of inhaling the calming aroma while engaging in play provides a dual focus.
6. As your child molds, shapes, and creates, engage them in conversation about the textures they feel and the scents they smell. Doing so will help enhance their sensory experience, build their vocabulary, and help them express themselves.
7. You can introduce challenges like, *"Can you make a shape that represents how you feel today?"* or *"Can you mold something that you wish to dream about tonight?"* This keeps their concentration anchored to the task while subtly introducing emotional awareness.

8. After playtime, store the playdough in an airtight container. You can revisit this activity multiple times, each session building upon the previous, allowing children to develop their concentration and sensory exploration skills further.

Processing the Activity:
- Discuss the feelings they experienced while playing with the scented playdough. *Did they feel calm, relaxed, more focused? Did the aroma make a difference in how they felt?*
- Encourage them to use the playdough as a tool whenever they feel overwhelmed or distracted. The molding combined with the calming scent can serve as a grounding technique.

Calming Glitter Jar

In the bustling world of a child's imagination, emotions can often feel like a tornado of thoughts, sometimes clear and at other times chaotic. The Calming Glitter Jar is a beautiful embodiment of these whirlwind feelings. As the glitter swirls and eventually settles, children are provided with a visual representation of how chaotic emotions can find calm. It serves as a tactile and visual reminder that even amid emotional upheaval, a calm center can be found.

Objective:
- To offer a visual and hands-on tool that helps children focus and find calm.
- To provide a metaphorical representation of how turbulent feelings can settle with time and patience.
- To enhance concentration through a mesmerizing sensory experience.

Best Suited For:
Children aged 3 to 9, particularly those who face challenges in managing overwhelming emotions, benefit from visual aids or sensory-based activities to find calm and focus.

Materials Needed:
- A clear jar with a tight-sealing lid, preferably plastic, for safety.
- Warm water.
- Fine glitter in multiple colors.
- Clear liquid glue or glitter glue.
- Optional: food coloring for added effect.

Instructions:
1. Begin by filling the jar about three-quarters full with warm water.
2. Invite your child to choose their favorite glitter colors. The colors can represent different feelings or thoughts. For instance, blue might represent sadness, gold could represent happiness, and red might represent anger. Allow them to sprinkle a generous amount of glitter into the jar.
3. Add a few drops of clear liquid glue or a blob of glitter glue to the mix. This helps the glitter to swirl and settle more slowly, extending the calming effect.
4. Optionally, you can add a drop or two of food coloring if your child wants the water to have a hue. It adds depth to the swirling effect, but it's essential not to overdo it, as you still want the glitter to be visible.
5. Seal the jar tightly. Consider super-gluing the lid closed to prevent spills and ensure it is childproof.
6. Once sealed, shake the jar well and watch the glitter swirl. Sit with your child and watch as the glitter starts to settle. Compare the swirling glitter to a flurry of feelings or thoughts and how, with time, just like the settling glitter, these feelings can find calm.

7. Use this time to discuss any feelings your child might be experiencing. Encourage them to talk about the emotions the swirling and settling glitter brings to mind.
8. Shaking and watching the glitter can be repeated whenever the child feels overwhelmed.

Processing the Activity:
- After the activity, ask your child about their experience. *How did they feel when the glitter swirled compared to when it settled? Could they relate those feelings to times when they felt overwhelmed or calm?*
- Ponder upon the colors chosen. *Did they have specific emotions in mind for each hue?* This opens a conversation about understanding and articulating emotions.
- As days pass, when your child faces a challenging situation, remind them of the glitter jar. Encourage them to visualize their feelings as the swirling glitter, knowing that those feelings can settle with a little time and patience.

Conclusion

Parenthood is undoubtedly a journey unlike any other, with its undulating paths marked by joy, challenges, discovery, and growth. Throughout your exploration, you delved deep into the core of play therapy, unveiling its profound influence on emotional and cognitive development. Drawing, dancing, crafting, storytelling—while seemingly simple, each activity has opportunities for discovery and connection.

From the promise of providing you with a comprehensive guide to understanding your child better through play to delivering on that promise with actionable insights and tangible activities, I hope you feel more equipped and empowered. Armed with the tools and knowledge from this book, I trust you will navigate the maze of emotions and experiences with confidence, understanding, and love.

But if there is one core message, one pivotal essence I hope resonates with you, it is this: The heart of parenting lies in connection. Beyond the strategies, the techniques, and the activities, the true magic unfolds when we genuinely connect with our children. It is in the shared laughter while crafting, the understanding glance during a storytelling session, or the mutual sense of accomplishment after a playful activity. These moments, however fleeting, build the foundation of trust, love, and mutual respect.

As you close this book and look towards the days ahead, I urge you to prioritize these connections. Let the activities herein not be mere tasks to tick off but cherished moments to delve deeper into your child's world. Remember, while the days of parenting can sometimes feel long, the years are indeed short. So, seize every opportunity to understand, play, laugh, and, most importantly, love.

Techniques, Tips, & Activities Recap

The following techniques, tips, and activities are found in *"The Play Therapy Playbook for Parents"*:

#	Technique / Hack	Explanation
1	Sanitize toys and play materials regularly	Maintain an organized space.
2	Ensure appropriate furniture	Furniture should be of the right size, without sharp edges, and stable to prevent tipping over. Ensure shelves or wall hangings are securely fixed and cannot be easily pulled down.
3	Inspect toys for breakages	Regularly check toys for breakages, as broken toys can have sharp edges, posing a risk.
4	Address small parts promptly	Ensure that small parts from toys, which can be a choking hazard, are promptly addressed.
5	Create a warm room decor	The room decor should resonate with warmth. Use soft lighting, such as floor lamps or string lights, to create a serene ambiance. Calming colors like blues, greens, or pastels can evoke a sense of tranquility.

#	Technique / Hack	Explanation
6	Shield from external disturbances	The therapy room should be a cocoon, shielding the child from external disturbances. Use curtains or blinds to dim bright sunlight, and incorporate soft background music or white noise machines to muffle external sounds.
7	Provide a personal storage space	Have a space where children can store their personal creations or favorite toys. This personalized touch can make them feel valued and establish continuity between sessions.
8	Ensure insulation from external noise	Ensure that the therapy room is well insulated from external noise, assuring the child that their conversations won't be overheard.
9	Respect personal space	Every child has a different comfort level with personal space. Respect these boundaries, seeking consent before initiating any physical contact.
10	Use child-friendly language	Children may feel apprehensive about what they don't understand. Use language that resonates with their world instead of therapeutic jargon.
11	Address children's concerns head-on	Foster an atmosphere of trust by addressing children's concerns directly. Initiate an open dialogue where they can voice questions or misgivings.

#	Technique / Hack	Explanation
12	Provide clear, age-appropriate answers	Help kids feel heard and validated by offering clear, age-appropriate answers to their questions.
13	Engage in independent play	Demonstrate how to use available materials through independent play. This often sparks the child's interest and encourages them to join in.
14	Encourage drawing dreams	Encourage children to bring their dreams to life on paper. This fortifies their imaginative prowess and provides a platform to discuss and unravel the cryptic messages of their dreams.
15	Illustrate different times of the child's day	Build time awareness and enable self-expression by illustrating different times of the child's day in color.
16	Recreate special memories through art	Allow children to recreate special memories through art. This enables them to immerse themselves in meaningful shared experiences.
17	Develop spatial awareness through play	As children shape a clay figure or stack blocks, they inadvertently hone their spatial awareness, an essential skill.
18	Explore different textures	Let kids engage with different textures, as this can be both therapeutic and educational.
19	Enhance fine motor skills	Manipulating small objects like pinching clay or connecting tiny pieces can enhance a child's fine motor skills.

#	Technique / Hack	Explanation
20	Allow creative identity exploration	Give children creative license to conjure up new identities. This stretches their imagination and builds empathy.
21	Allow destruction and recreation	Permit children to destroy their creations and then remake something new safely. This allows them to explore the creative process and understand the transformative nature of change.
22	Provide a physical vessel for difficult emotions	Having a physical vessel to contain difficult emotions can help children feel more in control. This strategy empowers them to manage and understand their emotions in a tangible way.
23	Build a symbolic island with blocks	Create a symbolic island with blocks to provide perspective on feelings of isolation or loneliness. This activity helps children express and navigate complex emotions related to isolation through symbolic play.
24	Tactile building for new perspectives	Tactile building allows children to see isolation from a new perspective. By engaging with materials and constructing, they gain insights into their emotions and develop a better understanding of their experiences.

#	Technique / Hack	Explanation
25	Jar of joy for happy reminders	A jar of joy helps kids collect happy reminders for when they need an emotional boost. This activity promotes a positive mindset by encouraging children to focus on uplifting moments in their lives.
26	Recycled creations for artistry and sustainability	Through each recycled creation, children express artistry and forge a bond with the planet, learning the profound value of sustainability and the joy of metamorphosis. This activity combines creativity with environmental awareness, fostering a sense of responsibility for the planet.
27	Nature's artful elements on reused cardboard	Let kids collect and arrange nature's artful elements on reused cardboard, fostering creativity with materials easily found outdoors. This activity encourages a connection with nature and provides a hands-on experience in creating art using natural elements.
28	Transform discarded items into an obstacle course	Transform discarded items into an obstacle course to encourage creativity, problem-solving, and sustainability values. This activity promotes resourcefulness and teamwork while instilling a sense of value for repurposing materials rather than discarding them.

#	Technique / Hack	Explanation
29	Engineering an upcycled play space collaboratively	Collaboratively building an upcycled play space builds bonds while fostering resourcefulness. This activity involves teamwork and creativity, encouraging children to see the potential in repurposing materials for play and learning.
30	Use diverse art materials for insight into complex feelings	Use diverse art materials and tactile mediums to allow kids to gain insight into complex feelings in a developmentally engaging way. This approach provides a creative and expressive outlet for children to explore and communicate emotions through various art forms and textures.
31	Balloons with written or drawn emotions	Inflate balloons with written or drawn emotions inside. This provides a tactile way to contain feelings both literally and symbolically. Children can express and release emotions by interacting with the balloons, fostering a tangible connection between their inner emotions and external expressions.
32	Crafting as a valuable outlet	Crafting provides a valuable outlet for children to creatively explore, express, and understand their ever-changing inner emotional landscapes. This hands-on activity allows children to externalize their emotions, fostering self-expression

#	Technique / Hack	Explanation
		and a deeper understanding of their feelings through the creative process.
33	Miniature "feelings garden"	Let kids nurture their own miniature "feelings garden" to teach them empathy, growth mindset, and regulation skills. This activity involves cultivating a garden as a metaphor for emotional growth, providing a tangible representation of empathy and the nurturing of positive emotions.
34	Personalized time capsule	Have kids create a personalized time capsule to allow them to gather mementos and preserve present-day memories. This activity encourages reflection on the passage of time, providing children with an opportunity to document their experiences and emotions at a specific moment in their lives.
35	Container with objects representing current self	Fill a container with objects representing their current self. This encourages self-reflection and helps children establish a connection between their personal identity and tangible objects that symbolize their current interests, preferences, and emotions.

#	Technique / Hack	Explanation
36	Happy snapshots and art within view	Have happy snapshots and art within view. This promotes positive reminiscence and family bonding by surrounding children with visual reminders of joyful moments and creative expressions.
37	Repetitive nature of dance steps or routines	The repetitive nature of certain dance steps or routines ensures that participants build muscle memory. This dance activity not only encourages physical activity but also promotes the development of muscle memory, coordination, and a sense of rhythm.
38	Dance to cast imaginative shadows on the wall	Dance to cast imaginative shadows on the wall. This encourages body awareness, problem-solving, and creative thinking by integrating dance movements with the creation of imaginative shadows. Children explore the interplay of light and movement, fostering creativity and spatial awareness.
39	Manipulate light and movement for shadow shapes and stories	Manipulate light and movement to design shadow shapes and stories. This helps children gain a new perspective on storytelling and creativity, as they use light and movement to create visual narratives with shadows. The activity encourages exploration and expression through the art of shadow play.

#	Technique / Hack	Explanation
40	Take turns leading and following	Take turns leading and following. This teaches the give-and-take of relationships through the collaborative experience of leading and following in dance. Children learn the importance of communication, cooperation, and understanding within relationships, promoting social skills and empathy.
41	Freeze dancing breaks	Take fun musical breaks for freeze dancing. This teaches children to manage their energy constructively by providing a dynamic and enjoyable outlet for physical activity while incorporating a playful element with freeze dancing.
42	Listen to pulse for mind-body awareness	Let kids listen to their pulse at rest and after activity to build mind-body awareness. This activity encourages children to connect with their own body's responses, promoting mindfulness and an understanding of the link between physical sensations and emotional states.

#	Technique / Hack	Explanation
43	Emotional dance tag	Take turns leading in emotional dance tag. "Taggers" enables safe emotional expression and role play. This activity allows children to express and explore emotions through movement, fostering a sense of playfulness while encouraging communication and understanding of emotional states.
44	Adopting a character for emotional expression	By adopting a character, they can voice feelings or problems that they might find too challenging to discuss as themselves. This role-playing activity provides a creative and safe outlet for expressing emotions that may be difficult to verbalize directly, promoting emotional exploration and communication.
45	Understanding facial expressions	For children, understanding their facial expressions can be the first step in acknowledging and managing their emotions. This activity focuses on self-awareness and emotional intelligence, helping children recognize and interpret facial cues as a key aspect of understanding and expressing emotions.

#	Technique / Hack	Explanation
46	Record screen time	Write down the start and end times whenever your child uses a screen. This monitoring activity promotes awareness of screen time and serves as a tool for discussions on healthy screen usage, contributing to responsible and balanced screen habits.
47	Discuss and establish screen-free periods	If you find the screen time excessive, discuss it with your child and establish designated screen-free periods. This approach involves open communication and collaborative decision-making, encouraging children to participate in setting boundaries for screen use.
48	Be mindful of over-reliance on text and emojis	Over-reliance on text and emojis can reduce the ability to interpret facial expressions and body language. This awareness activity emphasizes the importance of diverse communication skills beyond digital text, fostering a richer understanding of non-verbal cues in interpersonal interactions.
49	Watch for signs of screen dependency	If your child becomes irritable or upset when their screen time is reduced or interrupted, this could be a sign of screen dependency. Recognizing and addressing such signs is crucial in promoting a healthy balance between screen use and other activities in a child's daily routine.

#	Technique / Hack	Explanation
50	Build a fort for problem-solving and imaginative play	Let kids build a fort. This offers them a special space that also nurtures their problem-solving abilities, spatial reasoning, and imaginative prowess. Building a fort provides a creative and constructive activity that engages children's cognitive and imaginative skills, fostering a sense of accomplishment.
51	Pause to admire nature	Pause to admire nature. This can be profoundly therapeutic for children. Encouraging moments of nature appreciation promotes mindfulness and a connection to the outdoors, contributing to overall well-being and providing a calming and rejuvenating experience.
52	Guided meditation for focus and calm	Guided meditation, specifically tailored for children, can take them on magical journeys, all while they remain rooted in one spot, enhancing their ability to focus and remain calm. This mindfulness activity introduces children to relaxation techniques, supporting emotional regulation and mental well-being.

Activities:
Drawing and Painting Activities

1. My Safe Space
2. Emotion Faces
3. Illustrating Dreamscapes
4. Rainbow of Me
5. My Day in Colors
6. Color Mixing Magic
7. My Future Vision
8. Memory Recall
9. Character Creations

Constructing and Sculpting Activities

1. Smash and Rebuild
2. Emotion Containers
3. Wall of Worries
4. Island of Isolation
5. Jar of Joy
6. Nature's Mosaic
7. Upcycling Obstacle Course

Crafts Activities

1. Emotion Balloons
2. Feelings Garden
3. Dream Haven
4. Heart's Canvas
5. Bonds on Board
6. Time Capsule
7. Memory Magnets

Dancing and Music Activities

1. Shadow Dance
2. Mirror Dance
3. Freeze Dance
4. Heartbeat Listening
5. Emotion Dance Tags
6. Emotion Soundtrack
7. Emotion Karaoke
8. Humming and Healing
9. Songwriting Therapy

Acting and Storytelling Activities

1. Facial Expression Mirror
2. Family Dynamics Role-Playing
3. Social Interaction Improvisation
4. Puppet Tales
5. Puppetry Emotion Scenarios
6. Personal Story Sharing
7. Emotion Fairy Tales

Digital Detox Activities

1. Nature Scavenger Hunt
2. Build a Fort
3. Bird Watching
4. Device Sleeping Bags
5. Screen Time Storyboard
6. Memory Mosaic

Self-Control and Concentration Activities

1. Breathing and Grounding Techniques
2. Sensory Exploration
3. Guided Meditation
4. Concentration Card Games
5. I Spy
6. Worry Monster
7. Soothing Scented Playdough
8. Calming Glitter Jar

References

Athena A. Drewes. (2013). *The Therapeutic Powers of Play: 20 Core Agents of Change*. Charles E. Schaefer (Ed.). John Wiley & Sons.

Cangelosi, D. M. (2002). *Play Therapy Techniques*. Charles E. Schaefer (Ed.). Rowman & Littlefield.

Division of Behavioral and Social Sciences and Education. (2016). *Parenting Matters: Supporting Parents of Children Ages 0-8*. National Academies of Sciences, Engineering, and Medicine. National Academies Press.

Epstein, R. (2000). *The Big Book of Stress Relief Games: Quick, Fun Activities for Feeling Better*. McGraw Hill Professional.

Espada, J. P. (2022). *Anxiety Disorders in Childhood and Adolescence: Psychopathology, Assessment, and Treatment*. Mireia Orgilés (Ed.). Frontiers Media SA.

Hull, K. B. (2011). *Play Therapy and Asperger's Syndrome: Helping Children and Adolescents Grow, Connect, and Heal through the Art of Play*. Jason Aronson.

LaVigne, M. (2020). *Play Therapy Activities: 101 Play-Based Exercises to Improve Behavior and Strengthen the Parent-Child Connection*. Callisto Publishing.

Milner, P. (2002). *Time to Listen to Children: Personal and Professional Communication*. Birgit Carolin (Ed.). Routledge.

Mohanty, P. (202). *Maze Puzzle The Analytical Game*. Amazon Digital Services LLC - Kdp.

Petersen, K. S. (2012). *Activities for Building Character and Social-Emotional Learning Grades 1–2*. Free Spirit Publishing.

Reeve, J. (2014). *Understanding Motivation and Emotion*. John Wiley & Sons.

Silton, N. R. (2018). *Scientific Concepts Behind Happiness, Kindness, and Empathy in Contemporary Society*. IGI Global.

Tomlinson, R. (2020). *Teaching Kids to Be Kind: A Guide to Raising Compassionate and Caring Children*. Simon and Schuster.

Exclusive Bonuses

Dear Parents,

I am thrilled to present to you five exclusive bonuses that are designed to enrich your understanding and application of play therapy. Each of these resources has been carefully curated to complement the insights and strategies explored in our main text.

- **Bonus 1 - Unveiling the Layers: Insights from a Play Therapy Case Study Analysis:** Dive deep into the complexities of play therapy with this in-depth analysis of a real case study. Gain valuable insights into the subtleties of child behavior and the therapeutic process, enhancing your ability to interpret and respond to your child's needs effectively.

- **Bonus 2 - Crafting Creativity: Station Ideas and Essential Setup Tips:** Transform your space into a haven of imagination and healing with this guide. Discover innovative ideas for crafting stations and get practical tips on how to set them up in a way that encourages creativity and therapeutic play.

- **Bonus 3 - Parents' Guide to Play Therapy Assessment: Understanding Your Child's Journey:** This guide is an essential tool for parents navigating the world of play therapy. Learn how to assess your child's progress, understand the therapeutic journey, and become an active participant in your child's healing process.

- **Bonus 4 - Grateful Reflections: A Journal for Cultivating Positive Thinking:** Embark on a journey of self-reflection and positivity with this gratitude journal. It's designed to help you cultivate a mindset of thankfulness and positive thinking, which can be transformative in both personal growth and in supporting your child through therapy.

- **Bonus 5 - Play Therapy Techniques: Mastering the Art of Healing through Play:** Elevate your knowledge of play therapy with this comprehensive overview of the top 10 techniques used by professionals. This bonus is perfect for gaining a deeper understanding of how play therapy works and how it can be most effective.

Accessing Your Bonuses:

Scan the QR Code Below: Use your phone's camera or a QR code reader to scan the code, and you'll be immediately directed to the bonus content.

I hope these bonuses will serve as valuable tools in your journey through the world of play therapy. They are designed to provide additional support, knowledge, and inspiration as you engage with this transformative approach to helping children heal and thrive.

Warm regards,

Krissa Laine

Made in United States
Troutdale, OR
10/22/2024

24038800R00096